BÉLA'S STORY
A Brave Journey Through Unforgiving Times

Rita Schinnar and William A. Meis, Jr.

Copyright © 2016 Rita Schinnar. All rights reserved.

Published July 1, 2016
Fallen Bros. Press
29403 N Enrose Ave.
Rancho Palos Verdes CA 90275

ISBN-10: 0-9976728-1-1
ISBN-13: 978-0-9976728-1-7

Cover and interior design: © Guillermo Bosch, 2016
All photographs are the property of the Schinnar/Izsák Archive and used with the permission of the Schinnar/Izsák family. No reproductions of these photographs are allowed without the explicit permission of the family.

Background photo on back cover, and repeating design *tchotchke* are adapted from a photograph by Rita Schinnar of the "Lady Justice" statue atop the courthouse in Staunton, Virginia.

Dedicated to Béla's grandchildren:
Amir Hans Schinnar and Tali Erika Schinnar-Mazzola
who loved him dearly, and to his three great-grandchildren
whom he did not live to see but who will get to know him
from this book: Adrian Lawson Mazzola, Eva Caroline Mazzola,
and Connor Adalbert Schinnar, his namesake.

Contents   Page

Chapter 1	A Disrupted Childhood	1
Chapter 2	The Apprenticeship	9
Chapter 3	The Luck of the Draw	14
Chapter 4	Never Give Up Hope	22
Chapter 5	A Second Chance at Happiness	28
Chapter 6	Looking Forward to Eretz Israel	36
Chapter 7	Tent City	44
Chapter 8	Horses and Ice Blocks	51
Chapter 9	Growing Alienation	60
Chapter 10	The Great Escape	68
Chapter 11	The Italian Episode	75
Chapter 12	The Imposter	82
Chapter 13	A Chastened Return to Eretz Israel	89
Chapter 14	A Furrier Again	96
Chapter 15	A Taste of the American Dream	104
Chapter 16	Haunted by the Past	112
Chapter 17	The Correspondence	124
Chapter 18	This Too Shall Pass	140
Chapter 19	Retirement	150
Chapter 20	The Last Fight	166
Epilogue	The Gherla Memorial	175

Chapter One: A Disrupted Childhood

Dos lebn iz nit mer vi a kholem—ober vek mikh nit oyf.
Life is no more than a dream—but don't wake me up.
— Stutchkoff, *Der Oytser fun der Yidisher Shprakh.*

Adalbert Izsák, nicknamed Béla, was born the third of the six sons of Stefánia Izsák, in the village of Gâlgău, about 40 kilometers from the town of Gherla in the county of Someș in Transylvania. Not the Transylvania of macabre legends, of Count Dracula, but the Transylvania that existed before the Great War, before the collapse of Tzarist Russia, before the collapse of the Austro-Hungarian Empire, before the collapse of the Ottoman Empire, and before the Great Influenza Pandemic—those cataclysms bringing death and destruction to that unique principality of East Central Europe nestled in the valleys of the Carpathian mountains.

In 1912, when Béla was born, Transylvania was a multi-ethnic, multi-religious tapestry of Romanians, Hungarians, Jews, Armenians, Austrians, Germans, Poles, Lithuanians and assorted other ethnicities that lived there in more or less comfortable harmony, going about their daily lives in blissful ignorance of the horrors the next forty years would bring.

Zoltán Izsák, Béla's father, was a man of slight build and medium height, with a prominent forehead, receding hairline and a black, bushy mustache in the style of the unfortunate Austrian Archduke Franz Ferdinand whose assassination in Sarajevo, Serbia, precipitated World War I.

Zoltán was a tailor who worked for the Austro-Hungarian military, cutting and sewing new uniforms for the Emperor's proud army. Although tailoring uniforms was exhausting work, it was steady work, so each morning when Zoltán would leave their small but modestly comfortable house and walk along dirt roads that were muddy in rain, frozen in winter, dusty in the heat of summer, he was confident that he would be able to support his pretty young wife and his rambunctious boys until they were old enough to go off on their own, and then he and Stefánia could rest and enjoy their many grandchildren.

Stefánia was an attractive woman, round-faced, with thick dark hair that she often wore pinned atop her head. She had a pouting lower lip, eyes wise beyond her years and long narrow fingers that, had she been born an aristocrat, would have been suitable for playing the piano but, given her humble station in life, worked well for kneading dough. She was somewhat taller than her husband and she was often pregnant, bearing Zoltán's boys within a span of just twelve years.

Béla would later recall how his mother baked bread and cakes and sold them at the village market. He would also recall watching her use a scale and vigilantly weigh the quantity of the flour and the quantities of the other ingredients for her recipes, and explain to her boys that prudently economizing on the inputs helped her increase the returns from the sales just a tad more. However, his fondest memories of Stefánia were from occasions when she was preparing to leave the house for official business with local functionaries, when she would wear her floor-length green dress with the long sleeves puffed at the shoulders, with beige lace collar, a matching green hat, and what she referred to as her 'kiss-my-hand gloves.' On those occasions when she was not selling her breads and pastries, Stefánia wanted to be treated courteously, in the old European custom whereby gentlemen would kiss the top side of a lady's hand when they met.

She made a ritual of the act of putting on the gloves. She would call out to her boys, "Go fetch for me the kiss-my-hand gloves." Then, she would deliberately take her time putting on the gloves, slowly fitting in the fingers and pulling on the fabric to stretch it over her hands and wrists, and explain to her sons why she needed to wear them whenever she went out. She wanted them to understand that being poor did not preclude commanding respect. This image of Stefánia, standing tall, resolute, dignified was vividly and permanently etched on Béla's memory of her.

All of her sons adored her and loved her even when she would tell them teasingly that she would gladly trade all her boys for one good daughter.

The Izsáks were certainly not rich, but neither were they dirt poor in the tradition of the rural life portrayed in the stories of Sholem Aleichem and Mendele Moykher Sfarim. They were religious, but not piously so, definitely not Eastern-European Chasidim like the ultra-orthodox from the *shtetl*—the men with wide fur-trimmed hats and long black coats, the women wearing wigs and the boys with their *payot* curls framing their faces. However, religion did provide the Izsáks with a cultural and educational guide, so when Béla was four years old he joined his two older brothers and the other boys from their village at their *cheder*, a traditional Jewish school, located in the near-by home of their teacher, their *melamed*—he of the long black beard and a stern expression that was usually betrayed by his crinkled, mischievous eyes and calm demeanor.

Béla first learned Hebrew letters and then he studied the Torah, starting with Leviticus and then the other books of Moses. The small one-room *cheder* would be filled with sounds of the children's sing-song chanting as they read aloud to each other, repeating by rote memory the Torah passages they barely understood. Again, this learning was as much an educational exercise as it was a religious one: Béla learned the Hebrew alphabet and a command of Yiddish to add to his speaking knowledge of Hungarian and Romanian. By the time he was an adult he would add passable German, colloquial Hebrew, and charming, convoluted English.

Even so, Béla was restless at school. Rather than concentrate on his lessons, he was more interested in watching carpenters build a new house or investigating how hauling wagons worked or finding out what happened to the child crying by the large spreading oak tree. In many ways he was a typical third child, born into a complex web of already established family relationships where it was a challenge to get Zoltán's or Stefánia's attention. Instead, he made friends easily with other village children and, when he was not in school, he and his friends often roamed through the village chasing stray chickens, pestering the goats or poking sticks at the neighbors' dogs to set them barking. Béla would have been a nuisance but his ready smile and infectious charm, later-life traits already evident at such a young age, kept him out of serious trouble.

Sometimes he and his friends would wander across the unplowed fields and into the edge of the beech wood, hornbeam and fir forests, venturing not too far in because there were wolves and wild boar and even bears to strike fear in a little boy's heart, but there were also thickets of wild blackberries and tall cherry trees drooping heavy with sweet dark red fruit ripe for picking. There were wild strawberries spreading out along the ground and, for a sharp-eyed child, wild blueberry bushes. After gorging on their wild-growing harvest, the children were never thirsty because cold, clear streams ran down from the mountains and, sometimes, on very hot summer days they would even strip off their heavy pants and coarse shirts and leap into shallow pools—quiet water where the streams formed a bend in their journey toward the Danube and eventually the Black Sea.

But then, in the fall of 1918, as the warm days faded and the nights turned cold, a pestilence spreading north and east from the Iberian Peninsula crept into the natural beauty of Gâlgău. Suddenly, a lot of people—men and women and children and babies—fell sick with high fevers, coughing and, occasionally, a violent nosebleed. At first, the country doctors and the women who acted as nurses in the villages confused the new sickness with a common cold and assumed people were suffering from an especially severe version of the virus that reappeared every fall.

Then sufferers developed sore throats, exhaustion, headaches, aching limbs and bloodshot eyes. Some also experienced digestive symptoms such as vomiting or diarrhea. Most made a full recovery, but mysteriously, many of those who recovered soon suffered a relapse, and they then faced severe respiratory problems. In some cases, these patients also experienced massive pulmonary hemorrhages. After death, pathologists found those victims had swollen lungs and oversized spleens. At the time when this new virus was first identified it was known as the Spanish flu. Now epidemiologists refer to it as influenza A virus that caused the Great Pandemic of 1918 that killed over 30 million people worldwide.

In Gâlgău, in those days when significant health care was not available to the general population, people were used to being sick. While the new illness made people cautious, they were not in the beginning overly concerned. Then, old people started dying in large numbers, then babies, then children. The *cheders* were closed. Public schools were closed. People stopped gathering together in large numbers. Still the virus spread. Then, relatively strong and healthy men and women started dying.

One warm, sunny fall day, when the leaves were turning red and yellow and golden brown, when the pumpkins and squash and root vegetables, turnips and parsnips and potatoes had been harvested, little Béla came home, more tired than usual, in a grumpy mood that belied the beautiful weather. The next day he ran a fever and he was coughing continually. So were his four brothers, including the new-born baby, Károly. Stefánia was very concerned.

Then Zoltán, on whom the family depended, fell sick and could not go to work. Stefánia became terribly distraught about how her family would survive, or even if they would survive. She was exhausted from nursing her baby, her other boys and her husband. Cold compresses for their fevers, soups simmering on the stove, breast-feeding the baby, bedclothes cleaned and changed. Then Stefánia also became ill. The situation was desperate. No one would come and help for fear that they too would become sick.

For three days, the weak and feverish Stefánia somehow dragged herself out of bed in the morning, still dressed in her clothes from the day before, and the cycle would begin again: Feed, clean, nurse, clean, feed, wash, crawl into bed for a few hours, stumble out of bed, feed, clean and wash. Half-delirious, half-determined, she made it through each day. A strong woman.

Then, just as suddenly as it had arrived, the sickness seemed to disappear. Everyone in the family improved. First the boys felt better and they were able to help their mother as much as they could. The older boys did the cooking and the heavy cleaning. The younger ones swept and tidied. Baby Károly was strong, his cries echoed through the house. Then Zoltán was able to go back to work. Stefánia's fever broke, and she stopped coughing. She perked up. The worst was over. The family would survive.

Two weeks later, Zoltán barely managed to make it home. He was sweating profusely, weak, feverish, coughing up blood. His eyes were red and sunken. At the door, he fell into Stefánia's arms and she gently lowered him onto the floor. The two oldest brothers, Lali and Feri, helped their mother carry Zoltán to his bed where he lay virtually motionless, too feverish to toss or turn, his breathing raspy, labored, erratic. Stefánia sat next to him through the night. Occasionally Zoltán would open his eyes, wild, frightened, uncomprehending. Stefánia laid cold compresses on his forehead, kissed his cheek, tried to comfort him.

Zoltán lived through the night, but in the morning, as the weak late-fall sun rose from behind the mountains and the chilly damp ground fog lifted from the low-lying fields, Zoltán stopped breathing. He was gone.

Stefánia was disconsolate. No husband. No father for the boys. No money. But she remained determined her remaining family would survive.

From that day on, at barely six years old, until he left home eight years later, Béla's life was very difficult. Stefánia baked more bread and pastries to sell in the markets, but the markets were not open every day. She was the sole provider for the family and there was a limit to how much money she could make.

During those years when boys like Béla love to play sports, Béla never had the proper shoes or equipment. Despite these disadvantages, he managed to become a decent soccer player by fashioning a pair of shoes from discarded soles, old packing cartons and pieces of leather and fabric from Zoltán's last collection of scraps.

One day when Béla with his homemade shoes trotted onto the dusty field where the village boys played pick-up soccer, the other boys laughed derisively. One Hungarian bully who enjoyed taunting Béla anyway started chanting, "Jew boy, Jew boy, no shoes, fool boy." Béla ignored him until he received a pass on the left wing, then he deliberately chose to dribble around, then through the Hungarian's legs. The Hungarian tripped and fell as Béla sprinted toward the net. Goal! Béla was triumphant, the other boys stopped laughing. They even began to choose Béla first when picking teammates.

Gradually, the family's situation improved a bit. Lali, the eldest son, left to apprentice as a tailor in Bucovina which was far away on the eastern slopes of the Carpathians—too distant to visit often or bring money home, but one less mouth to feed. Then, around the time her second son, Feri, left to apprentice with a printer in Bucharest, Stefánia stopped resisting marriage proposals from an older man smitten by her and she remarried in a quiet ceremony with only the family present. So, with Lali and Feri gone, there were two less mouths to feed and her remarriage meant there was a significant new income source, but then, less than two years later, there was a new mouth to feed, a baby brother for Béla, Yaakov.

Béla had an uneasy relationship with his stepfather, Samu Lazar, but mostly because he worshiped his mother and he had an understandable resentment that after finally becoming the eldest male in the family, there was suddenly a new man to claim his mother's affection and then another baby to occupy her time and attention. But this resentment never really had a chance to fester into open hostility because it was time for Béla to also leave and apprentice himself to a master craftsman.

As she had done before, when she sought vocational training opportunities for Lali and Feri, Stefánia again consulted with close relatives, with distant relatives, with her two sons who were already in training, but she had not found a suitable apprenticeship for her third son. Then, in the spring of 1926, Stefánia made contact with a Hungarian furrier, Tálosi Mihály, who was looking for a young man to apprentice in his successful shop in the nearby town, known as Gherla in Romanian or Szamosújvár in Hungarian, since it was part of Hungary before WWI and again during 1940-1944.

As was her habit whenever preparing to go out for some official business, Stefánia put on her 'kiss-my-hand gloves' and travelled by horse-drawn carriage to Gherla where she met with Tálosi Mihály.

It was a difficult meeting. The Hungarian was clearly a stern taskmaster, arrogant and demanding. After they finished their obligatory tea and Tálosi had presented his requirements for the apprenticeship, he slyly implied to Stefánia that the negotiations might proceed more smoothly if she were willing to join him in the back room where he could show her his collection of luxurious furs. Stefánia understood what Tálosi had in mind, so she deftly countered that if Mr. Mihály were willing to accept Béla as his apprentice, she might be willing to visit her son once he began working.

And so the deal was made. Stefánia signed a four-year contract with Tálosi to train her son as a furrier, a trade he would pursue, on and off, for the rest of his life. She returned to Gâlgău with the intention of never seeing Tálosi Mihály again, and with little fanfare but some genuine regret, she hugged and kissed her son Béla, and packed him off to work in Gherla, apprehensive that Béla might have a rough time of it, but happy she would not have to see the revolting Tálosi Mihály ever again.

But that was not the case.

Chapter Two: The Apprenticeship

A yid hot akht un tsvantsik protsent pakhed, tsvey protsent tsuker, un zibetsik protsent khutspe.
A Jew is twenty-eight percent fear, two percent sugar, and seventy percent chutzpah.
— Stutchkoff, *Der Oytser fun der Yidisher Shprakh.*

The apprentice system Béla experienced in Gherla was originally developed within craft guilds during the Middle Ages and was still prevalent in East Central Europe during the first half of the 20th century as a way for boys born without access to higher education, but especially Jewish boys excluded by law from many occupations or excluded by poverty from attending rabbinical training, to develop a skill valuable in the mercantile world.

The training that Béla received should not be confused with a contemporary apprenticeship or internship. Béla's life under Tálosi Mihály's supervision more closely resembled the original medieval system of indentured servitude that allowed little freedom and little money for the young apprentice during the length of the contract. Béla was fed meagre leftovers: watery *kasha*—buckwheat porridge—in the morning, thin, salty cabbage soup containing miniscule chunks of potatoes for midday, and two slices of black bread spread with often rancid butter and a sparse coating of sugary jam in the evening. He slept on the floor, under the worktables, amongst the fur dust and pelt remnants from the day's labor, covered by a thin moth-eaten woollen blanket to ward off the chill. His one treat was the endless supply of caffeine-laden strong black tea in the workroom's rusty iron samovar to sustain his energy and encourage hard work.

And so, Béla trained to become a furrier. Homo sapiens and their close cousins the Neanderthals have been wearing animal pelts since the dawn of known history, and the basic rudiments of the furrier's trade that Béla was learning—scraping, stretching, treating, cutting and sewing the pelts of mammals, from humble rabbits to coarse muskrat to sleek foxes—is one of the oldest crafts practiced by humanoids. However, once we humans began to weave cloth made from plants—cotton and linen—or from animal products—wool and silk—or in more modern times, synthetics, wearing fur evolved from a basic necessity of everyone's wardrobe into a luxury item reserved for the rich and privileged. At that point in the history of fashion, the marketing and promotion of fur became as essential to the craft of the furrier as the technical aspects of creating the fur products. Tálosi Mihály only intended to teach Béla the technical work, but Béla, being a sharp and charming boy, quickly understood where the real money was to be made.

Among Tálosi's most important clients was the wife of Gherla's richest Armenian civil engineer and architect. Her name was Silvia, and she and her daughter Lena would often stop by the shop and examine Tálosi's recent arrivals of Siberian sable, Norwegian silver fox or Canadian beaver. If they were in a buying mood, they would negotiate prices for a new coat, jacket or throw while sipping Darjeerling tea and nibbling Hungarian sweet cakes—*malna piskotatekercs* or *dobosch torte*. Both women were very beautiful, but it was the young raven-haired, doe-eyed, curvaceous Lena who inflamed Tálosi's lust, although he managed to control his emotions in order to preserve his relationship with such valuable clients.

One chilly afternoon, when Béla had been an apprentice long enough to acquire a basic level of Tálosi's trust, he was ordered to bring furs from storage so that Tálosi could show them to Silvia and Lena, and then he was told to serve the special tea and cakes for the women's enjoyment while they were examining the furs. At one point, when Béla was clearing away the small china plates used for serving that day's selection of cakes and Tálosi had momentarily been summoned to the front of the shop, Silvia engaged the pleasant-looking teenage Béla in small talk, asking him how he liked working for Tálosi and how his training was going.

Béla was surprised that the matron spoke to him, although he was delighted to be able to dally for a while in the presence of mother and daughter so he could observe the lovely young Lena. However, when Tálosi returned and realized Béla had been speaking to the two women, he was furious. He admonished Béla for impertinence and immediately banished him to the shop's workroom.

On subsequent visits, the women managed to somehow speak with Béla, if only briefly. Béla was enchanted and unreasonably hopeful that he could somehow spend time alone with Lena who, at least in Béla's imagination, seemed to flirt with him by holding his gaze for a few seconds longer than necessary.

On one occasion, when Silvia and Lena stopped by the shop, Tálosi was not there. Silvia asked to see an example of Béla's workmanship, and Béla showed her a sable collar he had crafted. She asked to see more and so he also presented a mink cuff. Lena spoke softly to her mother while staring directly into Béla's eyes, "These are so soft, so beautiful. I love them." Béla was proud but flustered by her attention.

Silvia spoke to Béla, "These are lovely! You have learned quickly." She paused, and, then, in a secretive manner carefully asked, "Do you think you could make a few small things, collars, cuffs, trim for us? We would be so grateful."

"Of course," said Béla. "If you talk to Mr. Mihály…"

Silvia interrupted. "I meant just a few little things. Mr. Mihály doesn't need to know. We could even pay you. A token. To show our appreciation."

And so, Béla began creating, on his own time very late at night, small fur trimmings fashioned from leftover remnants scattered across the workroom floor. He sold these on the sly to Silvia and the beautiful Lena, and then saved his meager profits to send home to Stefánia. Unknown to Béla, the Armenian women often resold Béla's creations for a considerable markup to friends and family.

Eventually and inevitably, Tálosi Mihály discovered Béla's little enterprise. One morning early, before the shop opened, when Béla was eating his kasha and drinking his first morning tea, Tálosi confronted Béla. "You are stealing from me, Jew!" he roared. Béla trembled with fear and anger. He felt like he was back on the dusty soccer field at home, but in the shop there was no way for him to retaliate without endangering his apprenticeship.

Béla stifled his fury. "I am so sorry, *Tisztelt Uram*! (Dear sir), but I was only using the discarded pieces."

"Thief! Those were *my* discarded pieces!"

Béla bowed his head. "Yes, Sir. Those were your discarded pieces."

"You people are all alike," Tálosi hissed. "I will write your mother. She will come here and we shall see what can be done."

This threat was very upsetting to Béla but, again, he didn't know what else to do but to keep his mouth shut and hope for the best.

When Stefánia received Tálosi Mihály's letter informing her that Béla had been stealing, she was alarmed. Since the letter only said that Béla was stealing from Tálosi without giving any details and that Tálosi was considering cancelling Béla's contract, Stefánia wasted no time. The very next morning she left the baby Yaakov in the care of her fourth son, Sanyi, dressed in her formal green dress, pulled on her 'kiss-my-hand gloves', grabbed her hat and rode in the carriage to Gherla. Since she acted so quickly and her arrival was unannounced, as luck would have it, Tálosi was not in the shop when Stefánia marched through the front door, and so she had a few moments alone with Béla before Tálosi returned. As a result, she heard Béla's side of the story before she spoke with Tálosi.

When Tálosi met with Stefánia in his office, he assumed he had the upper hand, so he was blunt and crude. He said: "Your son is a typical Jewish scoundrel and a thief. I am inclined to cancel his contract and throw him out on the street. Do you understand?"

Stefánia was calm. She was prepared to negotiate, until Tálosi continued. "However, I am not like your kind. I am prepared to give poor Béla another chance." He leered at her. "That is, if you are prepared to give me a second chance with you." He ran his tongue along his lips.

Stefánia removed her glove from her right hand and Tálosi misinterpreted her action as a signal she was ready to comply. He lifted himself out of his chair and approached her, when suddenly Stefánia stood and slapped him hard across his face. As she stormed out of Tálosi's office, she grabbed her son by the arm and pulled him toward the front door. Then she gathered herself together, and spoke directly to Tálosi Mihály who was following close behind her, "My son is not waiting for you to throw him out. He walks out on his own!" Then mother and son returned to their home in Gâlgău where Stefánia made Béla a special meal of roast chicken and buckwheat pancakes to fill his empty stomach and help put meat on his bones.

Stefánia's heroic actions did not, however, solve the problem of what to do about Béla's need to train for a career. He still required an apprenticeship and he still faced an uncomfortable situation at home with his stepfather. Stefánia was forced to make a quick decision, so she sent Béla to live in Bukovina with his oldest brother Lali who was completing his successful apprenticeship as a tailor. Perhaps Lali could find something for Béla in a new, distant area where the rumors about what had happened with Taloşi would not have spread to the furriers of Bukovina.

It was late fall when Béla travelled by wagon from Transylvania to Bukovina, which meant he had to cross over the Eastern Carpathian mountains through the Tihuţa Pass, a hauntingly beautiful area mentioned in Bram Stoker's novel Dracula, renamed the "Borgo Pass" although the author never actually visited the area. Unfortunately for Béla, the pass, while not menaced by vampires, was subject to severe early winter snowstorms, and Béla was stranded for two days with almost no money in the cold and bone-chilling winds while the pass was being cleared of heavy drifts. There was an inn nearby where the proprietors allowed Béla to sleep on a hard bench in the kitchen corner to avoid freezing to death. It was uncomfortable, but Béla was used to the discomfort from his days with Taloşi.

When he finally arrived at his brother Lali's place, he encountered another difficulty—a disappointment he carried with him for the rest of his life: his oldest brother did not want him to be there.

Lali had his own problems. He was struggling with a craft choice that he disliked—being a tailor—and he felt that he had been pushed in that direction only because his father had been a tailor as well. He fancied himself in a more artistic occupation, and later in life he actually became a talented ballroom dance instructor.

Lali was also apprehensive about being Jewish in Bukovina. Although there were a substantial number of Jews living in Bukovina, the prevailing attitude toward Jews in this region that was part of Moldova and the Ukraine, was nowhere near as accepting as it was in Transylvania.

Whatever the reasons, Lali aggressively discouraged Béla from staying with him and strongly encouraged Béla to return to Gherla, humble himself before Tálosi Mihály and complete his apprenticeship as a furrier.

Béla, for his part, would never consider returning to work with Tálosi. Instead, he retraced his difficult journey back over the Carpathians and discussed different possibilities with his mother. At that time, Stefánia could think of no other options than to send Béla to Bucharest to live with his next oldest brother, Feri, who had apprenticed as a typesetter.

Almost immediately, Béla fell in love with Bucharest, a city that was experiencing its zenith between the two World Wars, known in Romanian as *Micul Paris* (Little Paris) for the broad, tree-lined boulevards, elegant architecture and a very cosmopolitan and sophisticated cultural ambiance. Although Béla, essentially a Jewish *Chayim Yankel* (hick) from the provinces, could not appreciate all that Bucharest had to offer, still, a young man like Béla—curious, charming, smart—could not help but be wide-eyed with enchantment. He spent almost no time with his brother in Feri's cold, damp, cramped tiny room above the print shop. Instead, Béla wandered the streets, supposedly looking for work but mostly soaking up the exotic attractions—glorious aromas of grilling lamb, the violins of the gypsy street musicians and the exciting rhythms of a strange new American music called jazz.

There were beautiful women dressed in the latest European fashion—shorter skirts, and blouses in bright, vibrant colors—and men wearing fedoras, silk scarves and slicked-back hair. The smart set often spoke French as well as Romanian, and the well-to-do were building villas copied from magazines with photos of houses in Chicago or Berlin. The city's population doubled from roughly 300,000 to well over 600,000 in less than ten years, as migrants from the disintegrating Ottoman Empire and the dissolved Austro-Hungarian states were swelling Bucharest's *mahalale* (slums) with immigrants desperate to find work. It was an exciting time, but a difficult time for a young man searching to find a new life for himself.

And then things became even more difficult when Feri was drafted into the Romanian army. With Feri gone, Béla would be homeless, so again, Béla was told to return to his mother Stefánia in Gâlgău where he would at least have free room and board, but again Béla said no. He was determined to remain in Bucharest.

During his adventures around the city, Béla noticed that Bucharest's newly rich haute bourgeoisie were acquiring a taste for expensive fashion and a number of furriers were opening shops on *Strada Blănari*, the traditional Furriers Street, and doing very well. However, there were many other young men competing for jobs and even though there was increased demand, Béla still had trouble finding work, at first. Then one day he stumbled upon Reich Furs, a business that had actually been established before the latest boom.

Béla entered and asked for the manager. It was Christmas season, the shop was bustling and he was told the manager was much too busy to talk with another shabby immigrant looking for work, but Béla was persistent.

Finally, a tired-looking, short, little Viennese man with a pencil-thin mustache, thick glasses and a *Hm-Hm* tic, either from nervous origin or adopted to project authority, was summoned to try and get rid of the tiresome young Jew seeking work. "Go away. There is no work," he told Béla dismissively.

Béla walked over to a display rack and removed a fine silk jacket with a thick luxurious silver fox collar. "Don't touch that!" hissed the Viennese fellow, who turned out to be the assistant manager.

Béla calmly turned over the collar and showed the assistant three flaws where the strips of the fox pelt had not been properly sewn together and explained that the fur would soon stretch apart and no longer appear thick and luxurious.

The Viennese manager was taken aback. He inspected the collar, then he observed Béla with renewed interest. "Where did you learn about fur?"

Béla explained his apprenticeship in Transylvania, exaggerating the length of his training and avoiding any mention of his run-in with Tálosi Mihály. The assistant manager, whose name was Max Schwartz, listened to Béla's description of his time in Gherla. When Béla finished, Max cleared his throat, hesitated, then said, "It's Christmas season. Perhaps I could use somebody. But temporary. Only temporary. Not much money."

Béla immediately accepted the offer. He was delighted. He had found work and, with his customary confidence, was convinced he would be at Reich Furs long past the Christmas season. And he was.

Later in life, whenever Béla would recall this episode, he would invariably remark that a person needs wits and skills to succeed in life, but ultimately needs also *a pintele glick*, (a tiny bit of luck). And in the second breath, Béla would espouse his other philosophy that *"Nu-i pentru cine se pregătește, ci pentru cine se nimerește."* (Good turns don't always fall in the lap of the person for whom they are intended, but in the lap of the person whom chance finds).

For the former expression, he borrowed a bit from Yiddish; for the latter he reverted to Romanian. It was common for Béla to punctuate his talk with a few chosen words or parts of a sentence from different languages, to communicate an idea or a punch line more precisely, he thought, or at least more beautifully, if the words rhymed nicely.

Chapter Three: The Luck of the Draw

Vos ken vern fun di shof az der volf iz der rikhter?
What will become of the sheep if the wolf is the judge?
— Kumove, Words Like Arrows.

Béla was a hard worker. He often attributed his continuing employment at Reich Furs after that first Christmas rush when others were let go, as being "because I had ambition to work."

While it's true that Béla had a very strong work ethic and he continued to develop his technical skills as a furrier, he was also retained because he had an engaging personality and he was quickly developing a knack for the marketing side of the business as well. Max, the assistant manager, initially antagonistic to Béla, became a friend and they made plans to open their own shop when the opportunity arose.

Those plans were temporarily interrupted in 1932 when Béla was, like his brother Feri, drafted into the Romanian army. After basic training, Béla was sent to familiar territory, to Transylvania, as many of the Jewish soldiers were. Béla served in the Northwestern city of Dej, the home of the Deyzh Hasidic dynasty since the sect's founding in the early 19th century, and years later, tragically, the site of the Dej Ghetto—a major holding area for Transylvanian Jews being deported to concentration camps in Germany and Poland. However, at the time, Dej was a comfortable posting for Béla, near his mother and three younger brothers in Gâlgău, and Béla's two years in the army passed uneventfully.

During this relatively quiet period in their lives, Stefánia also successfully arranged for her fourth son, Sanyi, to begin an apprenticeship as upholsterer, and for her fifth son, Károly, an apprenticeship as barber. Stefánia never had money to give her children, but she made certain that each of them was provided with a trade that would be useful to them for the rest of their lives; and in providing them with that opportunity she felt she fulfilled her obligation to provide for her family's future. Only her last boy, Yaakov Lazar, the young son from her second marriage, remained at home while Béla was in the army.

After his service in the army was completed, Béla returned to Bucharest where he was immediately rehired to work for Reich Furs. At this point, Béla's life began to improve dramatically. He was able to rent a decent room in a nearby boarding house and, for the first time, Béla was truly independent, on his own and able to focus on his personal life. There were girls, there were nightclubs, there were parties, there was dancing, but most of all there was work. Lots of work. Hard work. And there was money, a little at first and then more to come.

Although the clouds of war were yet again gathering across Europe, and a great economic depression had engulfed the economies of the developed world, those were also the days when, paradoxically, East Central Europe was intoxicated with possibility. Change was everywhere. Borders were shifting. Transylvania, for example, was batted back and forth between Romania and Hungary, depending on the latest treaty signed in Bucharest, Versailles or Vienna. Cities like Warsaw and Budapest and Prague and Zagreb were growing in wealth and power while simultaneously being embroiled in strikes, cultural upheavals and building booms. The region's politics were shifting to the margins, with both Communists on the left and Fascists on the right gathering appeal. Kings were toppled. Democracy was promoted. Autocrats seized power. Romania became relatively rich, the seventh largest oil producer in the world and the second largest agricultural producer in Europe, and yet, turmoil and disruption produced 25 different governments installed during the 1930s.

In Bucharest, Béla and Max were concerned about this constant instability and the growing power of the fascist Iron Guard movement that threatened pogroms against Romanian Jews. One balmy autumn evening in 1937 when Max and Béla were sitting in the pub *Carul cu Bere* in the Lipscani district, drinking beer, reviewing their savings and making plans, Max suggested that perhaps they should leave Romania and open a shop somewhere else. Béla, being his usual adventurous self and excited by Max's proposal, quickly asked, "Where would we go?"

"Istanbul," said Max. "I have a friend who started a business there and he says there is a lot of money in Istanbul. The sultan is gone. Trade is booming. Things are changing. A new country. Turkey."

"But aren't they Muslims?"

"Yes, but this Ataturk guy is forming a secular state."

"Are there Jews in Istanbul?"

"Lots of Jews in Istanbul."

"And there's money to be made?"

"So I'm told."

However, when Béla discussed the move to Istanbul with his mother back in Transylvania, Stefánia was passionately opposed to the idea. She and Béla had developed an even stronger bond during Béla's army days in Dej and, frankly, she also appreciated the fact that Béla had a steady income and sent money back home to help the family struggling to make ends meet in Gâlgău. She pressured Béla to stay in Bucharest and he went along with her wishes.

A few months later, as winter was coming on and the fur buying season was picking up, Béla, supported by Max, approached the owners of Reich Furs and asked for a substantial raise. Reich Furs was doing exceptionally well, the local economy was on an upswing, Béla was a model employee, but the owner said, "No, perhaps the following year." That refusal provided the incentive they needed. In 1938, Béla and Max opened their own shop, BélaMax Furs, a few doors down from Reich Furs on *Strada Blănari* (Furriers Street). With Béla's skills as a master furrier and his marketing savvy and Max's management and accounting experience, the new shop was immediately successful.

Once Béla started to make serious money, he began to spend serious money. He bought a beautiful, spacious apartment in one of the newer, fashionable developments in Bucharest. Then he purchased from the royal garage a Chrysler Imperial sedan that had been formerly used by a Romanian prince, and he hired a chauffeur to drive him around town. The car was Béla's pride and joy and he loved to recall in later years how much he enjoyed owning that automobile. He also loved showing off to his mother how much he had accomplished, and he was not only able to send Stefánia even more money so that she no longer needed to sell her baked goods at the market, he also made occasional visits to Gâlgău in his Chrysler. Life was good.

On one of those visits in 1940, Béla became aware that the Transylvanian border had shifted again, and Northern Transylvania had become once more part of Hungary because of a treaty known as the Vienna Award. This change happened because, after World War I, Hungary had been forced to cede much of its territory to surrounding nations, a loss that caused enormous resentment within Hungary. That resentment was a major factor in pushing Hungarian politics further and further to the right. Eventually, the Hungarian Regent, Miklós Horthy, formed an alliance with Hitler's Germany and with Mussolini's Italy to recover what Horthy's government considered to be Hungarian Transylvania. This portion included Béla's childhood home in Gâlgău.

While this situation caused some inconvenience for Béla during his visits, neither he nor his family foresaw the enormous consequences of these shifts in international politics. In fact, because Transylvania's Jews historically identified with being Hungarian and remembered, with a peculiar sort of nostalgia, their relatively comfortable status during the days of the Austro-Hungarian Empire, many Transylvanian Jews hoped that their reversion to being citizens of a conservative, aristocratic Hungary would be beneficial, even with Horthy.

Therefore, Béla's conversations with Stefánia during his visits were not concerned with politics despite the fact that World War II's shifting alliances and the growing confrontations between the Axis powers and the Soviet Union were taking place along the borders of the Ukraine, Moldova, Hungary and Romania. Instead, their time together centered around Stefánia's concern that Béla had yet to marry and give her grandchildren. Sometimes she would even tease Béla about his success, chiding him that, "a successful man with a big car and lots of money should be able to attract a bride."

In fact, Béla had begun to think seriously about marriage. While he was still primarily focused on making BélaMax Furs an even more successful business, he did have his eye on an attractive, lovely young woman named Sári, who, truth be told, reminded him a great deal of Lena, the Armenian girl he first fell in love with back in Gherla when he was still in his teens. Although Sári was Jewish and not Armenian, she had Lena's big brown eyes, dark hair and curvaceous figure. Béla was smitten, but cautious, partly because Sári was very attached to her mother who seemed to be always present whenever Béla and Sári were together.

Béla took his time. He courted Sári for over three years, taking her and her mother out to dinner, on picnics alongside the banks of the Dimbovița River, or into the foothills of the Carpathian Mountains for long hikes through the lush forests and even an occasional visit to seaside resorts on the Black Sea. As his affection for her grew, he took to calling her Sárika, and he found that the time he spent with her took him away from his worries and problems—from the increasing anti-Semitic tone of Romanian politics and the stress of running a business during a war. She became his haven and his joy in a way that he had never experienced before and his happiness gave him the courage to finally propose.

It happened one evening in the fall of 1943, when Béla managed to take Sárika to dinner without her mother hovering over them. There was a bottle of heady Romanian sparkling wine. There were blood-red and snow-white roses. There was soft candlelight. There was even a gypsy violinist serenading the couple with a romantic Bartók folk tune that would forever remind Béla of his Sárika.

Béla reached across the table and took Sári's hand. "I..." Suddenly he was overcome with emotion.

"Yes, Béla?"

"Will you…" Béla, who was never at a loss for words, couldn't continue. He reached into his coat pocket and produced a ring.

Sári smiled. "I have been waiting for you to ask." She raised her face and looked into his eyes. "Yes, Béla, I will marry you."

Béla was overjoyed, and so they were married. Sári and her mother moved into Béla's large apartment and Béla and Sári began what they hoped to be a long life together, with children that would be the grandchildren Stefánia longed for.

Six months after their wedding, Béla planned a trip to Gâlgău to present his lovely new bride to his mother. The trip went smoothly although Béla couldn't help but notice that there appeared to be an increased military presence at the border crossing into Transylvania. Unknown to Béla, in March of 1944, Miklós Horthy, still the nominal leader of Hungary, had met with Hitler at *Schloss Kleshheim* as the Russian Red Army was pushing from the east toward the border of Romania. The German Fuhrer was determined that Hungary not extricate itself from its alliance with Germany as Italy had already done. Unable or unwilling to resist Hitler's demands, Horthy agreed to what was already a *fait accompli*—the Nazi military occupation of Hungary.

While all of these international intrigues were taking place near Salzburg in Austria, Béla and Sári, along with Sári's mother, arrived in Gâlgău, where they were warmly welcomed by Stefánia, her husband and Béla's half-brother, Yaakov, the last brother remaining at home. That night, Stefánia prepared a special dinner of *flodin* (noodle and cheese casserole), *pashtet* (meat between two layers of egg pasta, baked with shmalts), *kreplekh* (boiled stuffed dumplings), and *strudel*. She had also planned a larger celebration for the following day to which she had invited the entire village.

However, on the following morning, as the family was eating breakfast, there was a knock on the door. Stefánia returned with a telegram Max had sent to Béla: "Urgent. Return immediately. Police threaten closure over Russian imports." Béla turned and spoke to Sári, "We have to go back to Bucharest. Now. Today."

Stefánia was upset. "But you only just arrived. I'm just getting to know my lovely daughter-in-law. We need more time together." She wrapped an arm around Sári's waist. "Don't we?"

Sári nodded in agreement. She not only liked Stefánia, she knew it was important to her future to spend time with Béla's mother.

Béla sighed. He knew he couldn't resist the demands of both women. "Well," he said, "Alright then. Sárika, you can stay here while I go back to Bucharest.

Then I'll come back and get you and your mother when I've straightened out this matter with the police."

When Béla returned to Bucharest, he discovered that the real problem was that a rich executive in the Romanian oil business who had purchased a very expensive silver fox coat for his mistress had been discovered by his wife who then threatened to divorce the executive if he didn't return the coat. But the mistress refused to give up the coat and the oilman refused to pay BélaMax Furs. When Max had demanded payment, the executive went to the police and complained that BélaMax Furs was illegally importing pelts from Russia with which Romania, as an ally of Germany, was technically at war. It was a complicated matter, but Béla found that a few well-placed bribes and an acceptance that they would never get their money back, solved the matter for BélaMax Furs.

However, when Béla was preparing to return to Gâlgău to fetch Sári and her mother, he discovered to his horror that the border with Hungarian Transylvania had been closed by the new government, under the orders of Hungarian General Dome Sztojay who was appointed by Germany to run the country while it was under German occupation. No one was being permitted to enter or leave Northern Transylvania as German troops, in a lightening fast military operation under the leadership of the infamous *SS Obersturmbannführer* Adolph Eichmann, rounded up Hungary's 445,000 Jews and had them shipped out of Hungary, supposedly industrial workers to support the increasingly desperate German war effort.

Meanwhile, back in Gâlgău, there was another knock on the door, but this time it was Nazi storm troopers ordering all of the Jews in Gâlgău to report to the village square for formal registration. Since this was official business, Stefánia donned her green dress with the lace collar, her hat and her 'kiss-my-hand gloves'. At the square, Stefánia, with her husband Şamu, their handsome twenty-year old son Yaakov, and Béla's lovely new wife, Sári, and her mother were ordered onto transport lorries that took them to a nearby train station. That train took the family to the Dej ghetto where they boarded another train that took them to Poland where they were herded onto cattle cars and delivered to Auschwitz, where Stefánia was stripped of her green dress and her soiled gloves before she entered the women's showers, while Yaakov and his father were sent off to the men's showers, and the guards threw Stefánia's dress and gloves onto a mound of other discarded clothing, then dragged her gassed, lifeless, pale naked body to the crematorium and shoved her gloves into the incinerator.

(left) Béla's parents, Zoltán and Stefánia Izsák, with the first two of their five sons. Zoltán was a tailor in the Austro-Hungarian Army. He died in the Influenza Pandemic of 1918. Stefánia supported her family selling breads and cakes in the village market. She perished in Auschwitz in 1944. This is the sole photograph of the parents that has survived. Béla only saw this picture when he was in his nineties, so for the first time since age six he was reminded of what his father looked like.

(right) Stefánia Izsák and her sixth son, Yaakov Lazar, born from her second marriage to Samu Lazar. Both mother and son perished in the Holocaust in 1944. This is one of only two pictures of Stefánia that have survived. This is the only photo of his mother that Béla had with him (above) Stefánia's sons: Four of the six Izsák brothers who were reunited in Israel in 1965.

From the left: Béla (the third-born, a furrier), Károly (standing, the fifth-born, a barber), Feri (the second-born, a typesetter), Sanyi (known as Shoani, the forth-born, an upholsterer). The first-born brother, Lali, was a tailor turned-ballroom dance instructor. The particular trades assigned to each son depended on the opportunities that Stefania happened to find.

(right) Béla at age 34 in 1946. There are no pictures of Béla from any period preceding this one. They must have been lost because of the dislocation during the war. All the existing photos of Béla are from the years subsequent to WWII.

Chapter Four: Never Give Up Hope

Di velt iz sheyn nor di mentshn makhn zi mies.
The world is beautiful but people make it ugly.
— Katz, *Fun Folks Moyl.*

In early July of 1944, when rumors of the deportation of Transylvania's Jews reached Bucharest, Béla was frantic. After numerous attempts to find out what was happening in Gâlgău proved futile, Béla assumed the worst and fell into a deep depression. He stopped going to work. He stopped eating. He locked himself in his empty, large apartment and spent most of his time in bed. He knew it was a fluke and a miracle that he escaped what he feared was the terrible fate of his mother and wife. Over and over, he asked himself, "Why them and not me?" as he contemplated life's randomness, arbitrariness, and impenetrable sadness.

Finally, Max roused him from his stupor. He refused to leave Béla's door until Béla let him in, and when he saw Béla, he was shocked. "What are you doing to yourself? Do you want to die as well?"

"Perhaps that would be best," responded Béla in a flat, dull tone.

"Don't be absurd," begged Max. "If you don't care about yourself, at least care about me and about our employees. Do you want to destroy us as well?"

Max's comment roused Béla who assumed Max was referring to Béla's family in Transylvania. "As well!" Béla shouted, "What is that supposed to mean?" He leapt forward and swung a fist at Max, hitting Max on the side of his head. Fortunately for Max, Béla was weak from hunger and his blow did little damage. Max laughed. "So, you do still have some fight left in you! Come on, let's get you something to eat."

The two, who were by now old friends, left Béla's apartment and went to the *Carul cu Bere* where they discussed plans to save their business and their own lives.

And plans were necessary because the situation in Bucharest was becoming increasingly bleak for Jewish residents. During the years just before World War II, as pogroms and devastation swept across the traditional *shtetls* of rural Romania, the Jews of urban, sophisticated Bucharest had a relatively easy time of it. King Carol II was openly hostile to anti-Semitism, perhaps because Elena Lupescu, his mistress, and a number of his close friends in the Romanian government were Jewish, perhaps because Carol II was a genuine Romanian nationalist who was determined that his country not fall under the control of Germany and the Romanian proto-fascists of the Iron Guard.

However, by 1940, King Carol had been overthrown by Ion Antonescu, a Romanian military officer and authoritarian politician who became Romania's dictator during the war. Antonescu decreed and enforced despicable laws that were responsible for the deaths of tens of thousands of Bessarabian, Ukrainian and other rural Romanian Jews, but even Antonescu refused to enact on Bucharest's Jews the 'Final Solution' as it was applied throughout the rest of Nazi-occupied Europe. As a result, the Iron Guard accused him of "Jewish sympathies" because his ex-wife and stepmother were Jewish. Under pressure from the extreme right, Antonescu did allow Jewish businesses to be plundered and individual Jews to be imprisoned and sent off to forced labor camps. Béla's younger brother, Sanyi, was one of those sent to a forced labor camp, although he survived the ordeal and was released at the end of the war.

In 1941, the tension between Antonescu's government and the Iron Guard broke out into armed conflict. To legitimize their rebellion, the Iron Guard instituted a pogrom against the Jews of Bucharest. They attacked the Jewish boroughs of *Dudești* and *Văcărești*, set the neighborhoods on fire, stormed Jewish homes and synagogues, and turned the Iron Guard's headquarters into torture centers. Jews were randomly murdered, but there were also organized executions. Some Jews were thrown from the top floors of the police headquarters building.

Altogether, during the pogrom, 125 Bucharest Jews were murdered and 1,274 businesses, stores, workshops, homes and offices were badly damaged or destroyed. Antonescu crushed the Iron Guard rebellion, but harassment, expropriation and thievery against Jewish businesses continued.

However, throughout the war, up until that horrible summer of 1944, Max and Béla were somehow able to keep their business open. Then, on August 23, 1944, Antonescu was overthrown in a coup organized by the young monarch Michael I. The new king decreed that Romania was now fighting on the side of the Allies. Ironically, Bucharest was then bombed by the *Luftwaffe*, and the Romanian army suffered terrible losses fighting the German forces that were being pushed back into Germany. Freed from the Nazis but swept by roving gangs of thugs from both ends of the political spectrum, Bucharest was a very dangerous city. Béla took to living in various places, sometimes sleeping at the store, sometimes with various friends, occasionally with a Christian ex-girlfriend who was willing to shelter him. He was forced to give up his precious Chrysler Imperial—a loss that pained him out of all proportion to his more important losses, but the one final deprivation that seemed to signify that his life in Bucharest was becoming increasingly impossible.

One afternoon in October of 1944, when Béla was on the verge of entering a deli on *Strada Covaci* to purchase *mici* (traditional spicy sausages), a complete stranger warned him that one of the remaining anti-Semitic gangs was inside the deli searching for Jews to beat up. Béla turned and walked away from the deli as slowly as he could to avoid drawing attention to himself, but this narrow escape convinced him that he had to do something dramatic to finally end the constant tension and harassment. Without telling Max or any of his friends, he made plans with his cousin Magda, who before the war was a promising ballerina with the Bucharest National Ballet Company, to flee Romania and go by boat across the Black Sea to Russia.

Leaving Romania was not so big a problem. There were many small boats in the port city of Constanța that were plying the semi-legal and not particularly clandestine business of ferrying Jews out of Romania across the sea to Russia. The more serious problems for the refugees was the danger of the crossing itself in overcrowded vessels—the Black Sea is a very large, often turbulent body of water—and then the fact that Russia officially only accepted Jews from Bessarabia and Bukovina, regions the Soviets intended to annex.

In the cold and rainy twilight of evening, Béla along with Magda, her boyfriend and dozens of others, paid the captain of a small fishing vessel to take them to Novorossiysk, a journey of roughly five hundred miles over three or four days across open water still patrolled by German submarines in the west and Russian frigates in the east.

On that very first night, as the rain increased, the winds grew stronger and suddenly a violent storm swept down across the sea from the north. The small boat was tossed roughly across the choppy water as waves reached ten feet and water poured over the gunwales. Magda became seasick and vomited continually, unable to help the others as they attempted to bale water from the boat's hold so they would not be capsized and drowned.

Around daybreak, as weak silver sunlight gradually spread across the dark gray sky, the winds abated and the sea grew calmer, but a steady drizzle continued throughout the day and the following night. Everyone was miserable, wet and cold. The meager bread and hard salami and cheese rations the refugees had brought with them were waterlogged and barely edible. Magda continued to be sick and dangerously dehydrated.

Finally, on the morning of the fourth day, as they approached the Russian coast, the sun burst through the clouds, the sky was a deep azure blue and the water was as calm as a swimming pool. Everyone on board the fishing vessel took the change in the weather as a good omen that they had survived and would soon find refuge in a friendly country where they could begin a new life free from the turmoil in Romania.

As the captain maneuvered his boat away from the main commercial port at Novorossiysk, toward the smaller fishing village at Kabardinka, an armed Russian frigate approached. A uniformed policeman stood at the bow of the frigate and ordered the Romanian boat to shut down its engines and allow the Russian border police to search the vessel and interview the passengers. When it became obvious that the Jews on board were not from Bessarabia or Bukovina but from Bucharest, the police forced the boat back out to deep water and warned the captain that if he attempted to return to Russian soil they would sink his boat and send all those aboard to the bottom of the sea.

Béla again experienced an intense sense of frustration and despair. Again he decided that he didn't care if he lived or he died. He hauled himself up unto the gunwale and was preparing to leap into the water when an arm reached out and pulled him back into the boat. As Béla fought to release himself from the stranger's grip, an old man's voice whispered in his ear, "Young man, there is always time to die. No need to hurry it. Don't lose hope." As Béla turned to look into the old man's wrinkled face and tired sunken eyes, then back toward the sea, then again at the smiling old man, he experienced an epiphany and his mind latched onto a mantra of sorts that stayed with him for the rest of his life, *Don't lose hope.*

But as the disappointed, exhausted and haunted passengers disembarked back into Romania four days later, it was increasingly difficult to keep that sense of hope alive. For one thing, Bucharest remained chaotic, filled with turbulence and violence. For another, Max was disappointed that Béla had abandoned him. His disappointment led to friction between the two and their business seemed to be on its last legs.

During one of their meetings, Max told Béla that Béla's continuing dreams of creating a better life somewhere else was creating an impossible situation. Béla shot back that Max's determination to tough it out amongst the horrors of wartime Bucharest left him with no hope for a better future. Their quarrel escalated. They were shouting and screaming at each other. Suddenly, Max sat down and was silent. Béla stared at him. "What?"

"Let's end it. Let's dissolve the business," said Max.
"How will that solve our problems?" asked Béla.
"It won't" said Max, "but at least I can live in peace."
"There will be no peace if we stay in Romania," countered Béla.

But Béla was partly wrong. By the spring of 1945 the war was finally over and Bucharest was free of conflict. The rebuilding began. Because Romania had joined with the Allies in the final defeat of Nazi Germany, the Soviet leader, Josef Stalin, initially supported King Michael's government. Businesses that had been shut down by the Russian army when they entered the city were allowed to reopen, and for the next two and a half years Bucharest experienced a remarkable recovery from the devastation of its wrecked economy and mangled infrastructure. Max and Béla reconciled and reopened their shop under its old name—BelaMax Furs. Béla was forced to admit that Max's tenacity and determination to remain in Bucharest might have been the best attitude after all.

The end of the war also provided an opportunity for Béla to seek to discover for certain what had happened to his family back in Transylvania, but try as he might, the chaos of people moving back and forth across national boundaries, the destruction of records and the disruption of so many lives meant that getting accurate information was exceedingly difficult. Persons freed from the concentration camps were held for years in 'Displaced Persons' camps because they had nowhere else to go—their homes were destroyed or were appropriated by strangers who had moved in. The survivors—confused and exhausted, gripped with anguish over losing parents and siblings, their spouses and children, and enduring physical pains from injuries inflicted on their own bodies during forced long marches on foot, or hard labor, or the harshness of their living conditions in the camps, without proper food or clothing—were lost in the continuing disruption of normal life.

Then, by chance, while Béla was sitting in the *Carul cu Bere* with Max, discussing different ways they could market luxury furs when so many Romanians were only concerned with bare essentials, Béla spotted a familiar face at a table across the room. The man was staring off into middle space, and there was a flat, haunted expression in his sunken eyes, but Béla was pretty certain the man was Daitel Mișu, an old family friend from Gâlgău—a Jew whom Béla assumed must have been caught up in the mass deportations.

Béla cautiously approached the table where the man was sitting alone. He leaned over and touched the man's shoulder, "Daitel?"

There was no response.

"Daitel? Is that you?"

The man turned his head slowly and stared blankly at Béla. "Who wants to know?" he mumbled.

"Daitel, it's me, Adalbert Izsák, Béla."

"Béla?"

"From Gâlgău. You remember me."

"Dead."

"Who's dead?"

"Everyone. From Gâlgău. Dead."

Béla sat down next to Daitel whose hands began to shake. Béla took the man's hands in his own, and focused on his eyes. "I'm not dead, Daitel. You're not dead."

Suddenly tears rolled down Daitel's cheeks. "Béla," he said. "Béla."

"Yes, Daitel, it's me."

"I was there."

"You were where?"

"The camp. Auschwitz. Your mother, Béla, Stefánia. I saw her. She's dead. Your little brother, Yaakov. I saw him. He's dead, Béla. All dead. All."

Béla had assumed that was the case, but to actually hear someone say it, someone who had been there, someone who had seen and experienced the horror, was too much for Béla.

He rose slowly, barely able to stand. "Mama…," he moaned.

Béla staggered out of the *Carul cu Bere*. He left Daitel. He left Max. For a while, he left the world in all its ugly reality and wandered the streets of Bucharest in a daze, unable to accept what he already knew to be true. He could not believe that a God who cared for human beings would allow such evil to exist, and in that moment he lost all faith. He cursed God. He denied God. From that moment on, Béla never again allowed religion to play any part in his life. He also reasoned that the Devil himself would not do unto mankind what humans do unto each other. Also from that moment on, Béla settled on another existential axiom: "If I am not for myself, who is for me?"

Late that evening, he found himself in the Cișmigiu Gardens standing before the heartbreaking monument, *Izvorul Sissi Stefanidi*, by the Romanian sculptor Ioan Bârlad, depicting a mother, in anguish over the loss of her daughter, pouring water from an emptying pitcher onto the stones beneath her feet. But Béla could not help notice that in the park, all around this statue that represented the pain of losing a cherished one, there was an abundance of life: beautiful black swans swimming in Cișmigiu Lake, banks of red, yellow and bright purple flowers on the hillside, towering lush green chestnut and walnut trees that had survived, as had he, the bombings, the destruction, the death. Béla whispered to himself, returning to his new mantra, *Don't lose hope*, and with that declaration he affirmed his will to carry on.

Chapter Five: A Second Chance at Happiness

Az dos harts iz ful, geyen di oygn iber.
When the heart is full, the eyes overflow.
— Bernstein, Jüdische Sprichwörter und Redensarten.

Life in Bucharest before December 30, 1947, when King Michael was forced to abdicate and leave the country for exile in London, provided a relatively prosperous two years for Béla. Although he was not able to reclaim his beloved Chrysler Imperial, he was able to once again live in his elegant, spacious apartment. His furrier business in partnership with Max was once again thriving. Only his loneliness, a haunting sense of overwhelming loss, and a certain guilt that he had survived while so many others had died, dampened his newfound hope.

Meanwhile, far away from Béla, in the small town of Fălticeni in the Moldavian region of Romania—a town that before the war stood as an example of a successful Jewish community in northeastern Romania—a once happy, relatively comfortable family was struggling against all odds to reconstruct their pre-war life. Their seemingly never-ending, miserable nightmare would come to have a profound and lasting connection with Béla.

The family's beautiful young daughter, Fanny Feldman, had been born during the good times when her family lived in their own house, on their own land and ran their own grocery store in Fălticeni. Their long narrow property, nearly identical to the properties of their surrounding friends and relatives, spread out like a line of railroad cars from the street to the full green chestnut trees and untended forest behind. The Feldman's grocery faced onto the dirt and gravel road at the front of the house, followed by the living quarters, followed by storage sheds and an outhouse, followed by a small parcel of land for gardening and keeping small animals. Each morning, all the families along and across the road would open a shoe store, or a bakery, a dry goods shop, a grocery, a butcher shop, or a tailoring business and greet each other in a virtual parody of the small-town, idyllic mercantile life lived by thousands of Jews before their world became the killing ground for the German, Hungarian, Romanian and Russian armies that swept back and forth across East Central Europe in a murderous, destructive rage.

Near the end of that war, in the spring of 1944, when word reached Fălticeni that German tanks, armored cars and infantry were approaching, as they advanced to reinforce the Eastern Front to oppose the Soviet forces, panic spread throughout the Jewish community—understandably so since everyone had heard about the deportation of Jews taking place in Hungary. Fanny's mother and father ran to the schoolyard and brought Fanny and her older brother Aşu, younger brother Nelu, and younger sister Suca home, where they hurriedly packed a donkey cart with a few belongings and their dog, left behind their house and all its contents, and fled without any clear idea of where they were going or what they would do.

Outside Fălticeni, the overloaded donkey collapsed and the Feldmans—mother, father and four children—were forced to trek forward on foot, shedding belongings along the way that were too burdensome to carry. As night fell, little Suca was frightened and exhausted. "Where will we sleep?" she asked.

Her father looked across the fields seeking some sort of shelter. He pointed toward a grove of willows near a small stream. "Under those trees," said Avraham, as optimistically as possible.

Fanny tried to be positive, as was her nature, but she was also scared and hungry. Tears formed at the corners of her sleepy eyes. "Let's just go back home," she begged.

"Maybe someday," said her mother, Malvina, trying to comfort her, "But not tonight. Tonight will be like…like camping."

But Fanny was not a stupid girl. She knew that whatever was happening, it was not like camping.

Their trek continued for several more days, as they forced themselves to keep moving away from the German troops. Eventually they reached the much larger town of Suçeava, a city that had once been the capital of the ancient principality of Moldavia. Avraham and Malvina decided Suçeava was large enough to provide them with a certain amount of anonymity, so Avraham went searching, discovered an abandoned dwelling on the outskirts of town and moved the family into the derelict old house.

"But who lives here?" asked Suca.

"We do," said Avraham.

"This is our new home," said Malvina.

But Fanny was not a stupid girl, and she knew this dirty little house with its shattered windows, broken down door and busted furniture strewn about in scattered piles was not their home. Still, she was willing, as was her nature, to make the best of it.

It was during their stay in Suçeava that Fanny grew from being a pretty young girl into a beautiful young woman. Her mother and father watched her transformation with some fear and trepidation because they knew that their eldest daughter was especially vulnerable during wartime. They made sure she was dressed as inconspicuously as possible in drab, oversized skirts and worn, unappealing blouses. However, they could not really disguise their daughter's attractiveness, so when the news spread that the fortunes of war had changed again and Russian troops were now pushing into Romania near Suçeava, Fanny's parents decided to move again because the Russians, known for their wonderful singing as they marched, also had a reputation, deserved or not, for raping desirable young women.

So the Feldmans moved even further north and west to Botoşani, away from the Russian advance that was turning south toward Bucharest. Fanny's Aunt Liza and her husband lived in Botoşani, so the Feldmans were able to live with Liza under extremely cramped conditions for the next nine months and then, in the late spring of 1945, as the war ended, the family decided it was safe to return to Fălticeni.

Safe, perhaps, but Fălticeni was no longer the idyllic place the Feldmans had dreamed about while they were away. For one thing, their abandoned home had been occupied by others, just as they had lived in an abandoned home in Suçeava. Those who had occupied their Fălticeni home had left it in a sad state of careless disrepair, and the intruders had removed the furniture, the rugs and the kitchenware to take with them to some unknown destination.

Moreover, unlike the situation in Bucharest, small towns like Fălticeni lacked the infrastructure and capital to quickly rebuild. There was virtually no economic activity, no commerce, no way to make a living. Instead, families formed small cooperatives, Sáring their different skills and meager assets to eke out a subsistence-level existence. They planted gardens. They foraged in the forest. They traded what goods they could make or purchase on the black market. They were often hungry and always worn down at the end of each day. Yet, very gradually, the family's situation improved. The younger children were back in school and Avraham and Malvina were planning to re-open their small grocery when tragedy struck again. Avraham, who was only 46 years old at the time, had a severe stroke that paralyzed the entire right side of his body and left his speech impaired. There was no hope for him in post-war Fălticeni—no clinic or proper medical care—so Fanny was charged with the heavy responsibility of travelling with her father to Bucharest to consult a specialist.

When Fanny and her weak, shuffling father stumbled into the doctor's office to hear the results of the tests the Bucharest clinic had administered, she immediately picked up from the doctor's nervous expression that the news was not good. And her instincts were correct. "There is little we can do," said the doctor as he removed his reading glasses, folded his hands atop the papers on his desk and faced the young Fanny while ignoring Avraham, the prematurely old man who sat next to her. "Perhaps if your father had received competent care when the cerebrovascular accident occurred, but now…well…"

Fanny wanted to cry, but her recent life had been so filled with adversity that she had developed a stoic control over her emotions. "There must be something you can do."

The doctor shook his head in a gesture of resigned finality. "I'm afraid not."

"Nothing?"

"Make him as comfortable as possible until…" The doctor left his last words unsaid, but Fanny was a perceptive young woman and she knew what the doctor implied.

So, a very sad Fanny and her unfortunate father returned to Fălticeni with the bad news. Since Avraham was incapacitated, the burden of supporting the family fell to Fanny's oldest brother, Aşu, who was forced to leave school and take his father's place in the cooperative.

Aşu worked very hard, but the family's situation in Fălticeni simply couldn't improve quickly enough to provide a decent life for a family of six. Therefore, Fanny, still only 16, was sent to Bucharest to live with her uncle, Nenea Sami—brother of Fanny's mother and a typesetter by profession—and his wife, Tanti Betty. Since this couple was childless and was relatively well-off, Fanny would be able to finish off her schooling there.

Sami and Betty were descent enough people and generous enough to accept Fanny into their lives, but, truth be told, they didn't really want the inconvenience and responsibility of caring for a teenage girl. One night, after Fanny had gone to bed and was presumably asleep, she heard her aunt and uncle speaking softly in the kitchen.

"She's always in my way," complained Tanti Betty.

"She's getting too much attention from that boy next door," said Nenea Sami.

"We can't live the way we used to," grumbled Tanti Betty.

"What if she gets in trouble?" said Nenea Sami, "What am I supposed to do?"

"Actually, she's a good girl," said Tanti Betty.

"Yes," agreed Sami, "but still…"

There was silence for a few minutes. Fanny had overheard their nitpicking before and she was drifting off to sleep when she heard Nenea Sami say: "A friend of mine, a typesetter named Feri Izsák, a good man, works at a print shop close by…"

"Yes…what about him?"

"He has a younger brother, a rich guy, lives in a fancy apartment, a furrier, I think…"

"So?"

"Well, this guy lost his wife in…umm, in one of those…those places…you know, she…she never came back…"

Betty lowered her eyes. "*May got annemen ir blut* (May God avenge her blood)…"

"Anyway…"

"He's rich, unmarried. Perhaps he would be interested in…"

"Ah, I see, Sami. Yes, speak to this Feri."

"I will do that," he said somewhat hesitantly, for after all Fanny had only just turned 17. Then he spoke more firmly: "Yes, I will do that."

Fanny was a smart girl. She understood what was being proposed, and she tossed and turned, ricocheting between fear and excitement for the rest of that night.

Soon after, Fanny's Uncle Sami and Béla's brother Feri discussed the possibility of an arrangement, a *shiduch* (match-making), with little or no consideration of either Béla's or Fanny's true feelings. However, it is doubtful that a 34-year old man, still grieving for his lost wife, and a 17-year old girl from the countryside, both of them recovering from the trauma of a terrible war, would have had a clear understanding of their feelings, anyway. At the most basic level, Béla saw a very beautiful young woman with whom he could have a second chance, a chance to start married life over again; Fanny saw a pleasant-enough older man with, she was told, an elegant apartment with indoor plumbing and his own prosperous business. Thus, after the initial introductions, the relationship was proceeding forward without serious problems, until suddenly there appeared two bumps in the road.

When Fanny's older brother Aşu, back in Fălticeni, heard what his Nenea Sami and Tanti Betty were planning for his younger sister, he was very upset. He immediately dropped everything he was doing and travelled to Bucharest to try and persuade Fanny that she should not marry, especially a much older man, simply because she didn't want to be a burden on her family.

He arrived at his uncle's apartment late on a Saturday night only to discover that Fanny wasn't there. She was out on a date with Béla. Aşu was furious with Sami and Betty. "How can you do this to Fanny?" he yelled. "And you let her stay out this late with this…this…" Words failed him. He sighed and shook his head. "Is she even coming home?"

Sami tried to placate him. "Aşu, this Béla Izsák, he's a very nice man. Fanny seems to like him. He has money. He can give her a good life."

"She's only 17, Nenea Sami, what does she know about life?"

"She knows enough," injected Betty.

"What does that mean?" shot back Aşu.

Meanwhile, while this back-and-forth bickering was taking place, Béla and Fanny had arrived at the apartment, and Béla overheard the quarrel occurring in the next room before Aşu, Sami and Betty realized he was there. When he heard them mention that Fanny was only seventeen, a fact that had been hidden from him, Béla blanched. He stared at Fanny. "You are…only…seventeen?" he asked. Fanny started to cry.

When the others heard Fanny crying, they hurried to join her and all five stood there in embarrassed silence for a moment. Then Sami said, "Aşu, I'd like you to meet Mr. Adalbert Izsák, Béla."

He turned to Béla. "Béla, this is Fanny's older brother, Aşu Feldman." Aşu, deeply suspicious, glared at Béla until Béla extended his hand and Aşu finally shook it. "How about I make tea?" said Betty.

The ensuing conversation was actually quite civilized once Fanny stopped sniffling, Aşu calmed down, and Béla recovered from his initial shock. Fanny made it clear that she actually wanted to marry Béla. She was impressed with the glitter of the big city compared with the smallness of her life in Fălticeni, and she would never return home under the perception that she had failed to make a life for herself in Bucharest. At first Aşu scoffed at Fanny's revelations, but eventually he realized Fanny was being sincere.

It was Béla who remained the most skeptical about continuing a relationship and planning marriage to a teenager. Fanny was insulted when she thought Béla was rejecting her and they all thought she was going to cry again, but then Sami said to Béla: "Don't worry about the age difference. She'll grow older next to you…You'll grow younger next to her…Time will make the age difference go away…"

Béla considered the wisdom of this advice, and Fanny expressed the opinion that she believed her uncle's observation was her own as well. Betty brought out a plum strudel she was planning to serve the following day but decided that perhaps this was a good time for sweets, and everyone sat around the table enjoying the strudel while she brewed more coffee.

And so the impromptu family council concluded on an upbeat note. The engagement took place in March, 1946, and the wedding followed just one month later, in April.

By her nineteenth birthday, Fanny Izsák, née Feldman, was not only a wife, but a mother to a baby girl that she and Béla named Rita. For the following three wonderful, precious years it seemed as if Nenea Sami's philosophical prediction would prove correct. But events have a way of overriding even the best of promising intentions.

(left) Béla at 34 and Fanny at 17, registering for a marriage license at City Hall in Bucharest, Romania, in March, 1946.

(below) Béla and Fanny on their wedding day in April 1946. Standing next to Fanny on the left are Nenea Sami and Tanti Betty, the uncle and aunt with whom Fanny stayed in Bucharest. They married her off to get her off their hands. Standing next to Béla on the right are his older brother Feri with his wife and son. Both Sami and Feri worked as typesetters and it was through their acquaintance that Béla and Fanny were introduced. That Béla was well-to-do at that time is evident by the mink fur jacket that he made for his young bride for the occasion.

(above) Béla, Fanny and Rita in October, 1950, the last picture of the family in Bucharest, Romania.

(below) Béla, Fanny and Rita in 1952: the anxious faces of immigrants in Israel still living in Tent City

Chapter Six: Looking Forward to Eretz Israel

A nayer meylekh mit naye gzeyres, a nay yor mit naye aveyres.
A new king with new decrees, a new year with new misdeeds.
— Stutchkoff, *Der Oytser fun der Yidisher Shprakh.*

After World War II, Bucharest experienced a significant influx of Jews as surviving refugees arrived from the concentration camps as well as from Transylvania, Bessarabia and Bukovina where they continued to feel unsafe. By 1947, the Jewish population of Bucharest had grown to over 150,000 and this thriving community was generally optimistic about their future. Bucharest's chief rabbi, Mozes Rosen, seemed particularly adept at coping with the confusing peculiarities of Romanian official policy.

But Béla's and Fanny's lives as well as the lives of all the Jews in post-war Bucharest were actually more precarious than they realized. After all, Romania had been an ally of Germany during most of World War II, and even King Michael's coup against the fascist Antonescu and the Iron Guard, and his subsequent support of the Allies near the end of the war, couldn't prevent the Soviet army's occupation of Romania. King Michael really had no choice in the matter. That occupation was agreed to by US President Franklin D. Roosevelt, British Prime Minister Winston Churchill and Soviet Premier Joseph Stalin when they met at Yalta in 1945 and placed Romania within the Soviet sphere of influence.

Although Stalin did initially allow King Michael's government to re-establish a pro-capitalist democracy in Romania, the heavy-handed presence of Russian troops created a political climate that was very favorable to the Communist party. The Parliamentary elections in 1946 brought them to power, and the Communists managed to quickly establish themselves as the dominant political force in post-war Romania. By the end of 1947, they were able to force King Michael's abdication and they then declared the People's Republic of Romania.

While these events were taking place, Béla spent his time as he always had, working diligently with Max to ensure that their furrier business maintained the amazing success they had experienced since the war ended. Wars are profitable for manufacturers, traders and suppliers and so there were plenty of rich Romanians who had a lot of money. One way they could enjoy their wealth was to buy expensive, exotic furs, and Béla and Max were among the best furriers in Bucharest.

The rhythm of Béla's and Fanny's shared life brought great satisfaction to both of them, and their marriage of convenience became a solid partnership. For her part, Fanny enjoyed the comforts that her new status as Béla's wife provided her. She was able to buy her infant daughter fashionable outfits and to furnish the nursery with a crib and a dresser and a bassinet from Bucharest's best stores. When she left the apartment and strolled along the streets, she had a fine rose-pink and cream-colored baby carriage and soft beige cashmere baby blankets to show off her pretty baby. She bought sausages at the Hungarian deli, chocolates at the Swiss confectioners and pastries at the French bakery. She had a full-time nanny, and when Béla arrived home tired and distracted from a long day at the shop, they often went out for a lovely dinner with wine, gypsy violinists and sometimes even dancing if the mood struck them. Fanny could hardly believe her good fortune after all the pain and suffering that she and her family had been through such a short time ago.

While Fanny enjoyed her new life of plenty and comfort, she was also curious and ambitious. She began spending increasingly more time around the fur salon, watching what was going on both in the showroom and behind the scenes. Gradually, she persuaded Béla to let her go over the books and she discovered she had a real talent for numbers, organizing financial information and applying other elements of basic accounting. Before too long, she had managed to develop better ways for keeping track of expenses and returns and, in the process, she discovered that Max had been skimming money off the top for years.

"Are you sure?" asked Béla.

"Quite sure," said Fanny.

When Béla confronted Max, he denied everything. "But Fanny ran the numbers," said Béla. "They don't add up."

"What does she know about numbers, Béla, she's just a kid. She should stay home and take care of the baby."

Béla was unwilling to become embroiled in an argument with Max at that time, but he could tell Max was lying, and he let Max know that he knew Max was lying. From then on, Béla always had Fanny double-check the books, and there were no more irregularities.

One evening, on a day when Fanny did not go to the shop but went shopping instead, Béla, who was almost always in a talkative, up-beat mood no matter how tired he was or how difficult his day, came home tight-lipped and nervous. At first Fanny thought Béla must have been fighting with Max. But she noticed that he angrily tossed that evening's newspaper onto the credenza in the entryway. She also noticed how absent-mindedly he pecked her on the cheek and that he retired to his study without spending any time with little Rita. When Béla hadn't left his study after a few hours, Fanny picked up the paper and out of curiosity checked to see if she could determine what might be upsetting Béla.

Initially, she didn't see anything particularly disturbing. Then she noticed a story that the *Adunarea Deputaților* (the Romanian Parliament) was considering a law that would nationalize Romania's large private companies and merge them with Russian cooperatives, creating large Russian/Romanian state-owned monopolies. There were also proposals to collectivize Romania's small family farms into larger state-owned and managed agribusinesses. This news raised concerns in Fanny's mind for her family in Fălticeni but, surely, thought Fanny, this couldn't be what was upsetting Béla. He and Max were small business owners. Who would want to nationalize their little enterprise?

The next morning, when Fanny asked Béla what was bothering him, Béla said there was nothing to be worried about but, over the following weeks, Fanny couldn't help but notice that Béla was becoming increasingly tense and irritated. Even Rita, still only a small child, sensed the growing stress around her and she fussed and fidgeted more than she had previously. Finally, Fanny could take no more. She cornered Béla as they were leaving work. She insisted they sit and talk, so they went to a small coffee house and Béla chose a table as far away from the other patrons as possible. Even then he spoke in an uncharacteristically low voice.

"I'm worried about what's happening," he said to Fanny.

"To the business?" asked Fanny

"To everything," said Béla.

"Everything?"

Béla glanced furtively at the tables around them and lowered his voice further. "The Communists."

"The Communists? But, Béla, lots of Jews are Communists."

"*Zey vet nit zeyn far fil mer* (They won't be for long)," said Béla as he switched from Romanian to Yiddish. That annoyed Fanny because she already felt Yiddish was for uncultured Jews, and she no longer saw herself as uncultured.

Béla continued: "The Communists might be good for the poor, Fannika, but they're not good for business. They will chase the rich and successful out of Romania. They've already got rid of the king."

Fanny sat back in her chair and sipped from her cup while she gazed off into the distance through the smoky blue cigarette haze that filled the coffee house. Suddenly she was afraid as memories of all her family's losses and constant moving overwhelmed her. She vowed not to cry, but her lower lip trembled as she spoke: "What shall we do, Béla? Will we lose everything?"

Béla had no ready answer and that lack of an answer frightened Fanny even more. Béla always had answers even when there were none.

Béla was, however, actually beginning to form a new action plan in the back of his mind and, as usual, his new plan involved adventure, scheming and commitment to the belief that his life would always get better. He was vaguely aware that around the same time that the economic and political situation in Romania had begun to unravel, events in the former British mandate of Palestine were evolving in a more favorable way, at least for Jews.

Although Jewish immigration into Palestine had been occurring in fits and starts from as early as 1492, when the Sephardic Jews were expelled from Spain, it was in the late 1800s that significant numbers of Jews migrated to Palestine. They were inspired by the Austro-Hungarian journalist, Theodor Herzl, who published two enormously influential books describing his vision of a future Jewish nation—*Der Judenstaat* (The Jewish State) and *Altneuland* (The Old New Land)—and is credited with founding political Zionism. Brutal pogroms sweeping through Eastern Europe during the first half of the 20th century produced additional series of *Aliyah* (waves of immigrants from the Jewish diaspora returning to "Zion" or the "Land of Israel"). However, it was after the horrors of WWII and the concentration camps when the massive immigration to Palestine occurred. Then, on May 14, 1948, the British Mandate in Palestine came to an end, and David Ben-Gurion declared "the establishment of a Jewish state in *Eretz-Israel*, to be known as the State of Israel."

Although the early years after the formation of the new Jewish state were hardly free from war and economic struggle, the idea of a "safe haven" for Jews had enormous appeal for European Jewry. Béla had numerous friends who joined various Zionist organizations that were being formed in Bucharest. Then, the Romanian Communist government hailed the first hostile steps. The *Securitate* (the secret police) moved against Bucharest's Jews by purging "parasite elements"—deporting the Jewish Zionists or sending them into internal exile in forced labor camps. Béla and Fanny had seen this happen before, all too recently, and their fears about their life in Romania increased substantially.

Then things went from bad to worse for Romanians with money and property. Business at Béla and Max's fur emporium fell off markedly and most of the rich customers who did appear in the shop were trying to sell their furs for cash, not buy new ones. And while Béla was trying to stave off economic ruin, Fanny set about dramatically reducing expenses. She had to let Rita's nanny go. Then there were no more trips to the fancy shops, no more expensive clothes, and no more nights out on the town. Many of the best restaurants were closing anyway. Still, Béla continued to struggle forward and not "give up hope," but for Fanny, her dream of a comfortable life with a successful man was fading quickly, and she began to question the relationship she had chosen in her naïve belief that everything would work out for the best.

In the fall of 1949, on one of those crisp, cool but sunny Bucharest days, when the leaves were turning red and gold and a clean, fresh breeze was blowing off the river through the city, on a beautiful day when living in Bucharest seemed the perfect place to be, as a toddling Rita held onto her mother's hand while they ambled down the sidewalk toward their apartment, Rita felt her mother stop suddenly, pick her up in her arms and hold her tightly to her chest. In front of them, a group of men in black leather jackets and official-looking caps were posting notices on the Izsák's apartment building. This activity was only mildly curious to Rita, but it meant a great deal to Fanny.

After the rough-looking men gathered up their remaining signs and headed off to another building further down the block, Fanny approached the entrance to their home and read the printed notices although she already knew what was written there: The government was expropriating their building. It would then be chopped up into much smaller multi-family units, with each family sharing kitchens and bathrooms. The last remaining vestiges of Fanny's luxurious life were being stripped away from her.

That evening, after they put Rita to bed and she was sleeping soundly, Béla and Fanny discussed their plans to join the exodus to Israel. Béla was excited at the prospect of a life-changing adventure; Fanny was cold and determined.

"We can start over again," said Béla, bursting with enthusiasm. "I can open a new shop in…,well, wherever we are, Jerusalem, Tel Aviv… Our life will be wonderful, just like it used to be here. But no one will threaten us ever again, and…"

Fanny shook her head. "No more dreams, Béla, no more fantasies. I am tired of shattered dreams. I am tired of…oh, I'm just tired. Once we get out of this mess, let's simply get on with our lives. They will be whatever they may be."

"But aren't you excited, Fanny?" He grabbed her by the waist and twirled her around, "A new life."

Fanny wrested herself away from Béla's arms. "Stop it," she said, angry and annoyed as she left, went into the dining room, put her head down on her treasured walnut table and cried silently for her lost elegant life. She was still not yet 20 years old.

The very next day, still excited by his ever-optimistic expectations, Béla went to the old, gray stone government building, not far away from the former royal residence, now the Communist Party headquarters. As he entered the lobby, he encountered a long line of people waiting to enter the offices where one could obtain emigration visas. The line moved very slowly. Garrulous Béla struck up a conversation with a small, well-dressed man with thin, steel-rimmed glasses and a neatly trimmed beard, and wearing a brown woolen overcoat and a yarmulke. "Going to Israel?" asked Béla.

The man turned to his wife, a small mousy woman also dressed in a heavy coat and wearing a hat and gloves. "Yes, we are making *Aliyah*," the man answered in Hebrew, "progressing toward Jerusalem." His wife smiled at her husband, an almost beatific vision on her face.

"What do you hear about prospects there?" queried Béla in Romanian, because the Hebrew that he had learned in the *cheder* in childhood was not very useful for ordinary conversation. "Good for business?"

"Business?" the man said disdainfully, "who cares about business? We only wish to live free in our Holy Land lost to us since exile." His wife nodded in agreement. "We will pray at the Wall and die in peace," she added.

Béla was somewhat taken aback by their seriousness, but another man on Béla's left side laughed deeply and said, "But we can't eat freedom, rabbi. I too hope we can make good business there."

Yet another man in line, a big bear of a man dressed in black trousers and long black overcoat, and wearing the fur trimmed hat of the ultra-orthodox and a thick, flowing black beard, pitched into the conversation. "It won't be easy starting out. These *komunist basterdz* (he reverted to Yiddish: Communist bastards)," he spat, "won't let us take anything with us."

"What?" said Béla.

"We can take all the Romanian *bani* (money) we want," the second man gave a hearty chuckle, "it is worthless paper once we leave."

"Better we bring gold or diamonds," said the ultra-orthodox, "and hope they don't discover them in our luggage."

The rabbi and his wife had tried to ignore the back-and-forth, but finally the rabbi said, "Trust, my friends, trust. In Eretz Yisrael we will be taken care of."

"We best be prepared to take care of ourselves," the second man joked ruefully.

Béla's Story

When Béla finally received his exit visas for the family, he found, to his consternation, that much of what he had learned from the gossip in line during his long wait was, in fact, true. He was even more apprehensive when he returned to see that Fanny had packed trunks and crates of china and crystal and silverware and furs and dresses and suits and toys for Rita and all of the child's beautiful clothes to take with them. He had to gather all his courage to tell her the new facts of their emigration. "Fanny," he said, I'm sorry but…" He tried to put his arms around her, but she wasn't in a mood for comforting.

"They won't let us leave?" she asked.

"We can leave," said Béla, "but…"

"But what, Béla?"

"Only two suitcases and, for some reason, two paintings."

"That's all we can take?"

"That's it."

Fanny didn't cry, but she did gather up Rita in her arms and fled to the child's bedroom. She slammed the door and slept with her daughter that night.

Béla was able to spend a lot of his useless cash to book a small cabin on the steamer Transylvania leaving in two weeks, and he purchased a few pieces of diamond jewelry that he told Fanny and Rita to wear when they were leaving, because he doubted the emigration officers would actually search the bodies of women and children. He also bought two paintings he was told would hold their value, even in Israel. He used his remaining cash to buy three solid gold coins he sewed into the lining of his heavy overcoat.

On a blustery, overcast winter day in late 1950, Béla, Fanny and Rita trudged slowly through yet another line as the Romanian emigration officers made one last check of the weary passengers before they boarded the Transylvania. Each of the émigrés wore as many layers of pants and shirts and dresses and jackets and coats as possible, to allow for more room in their two allotted suitcases. But Béla was wrong. The Romanians did discover and confiscate the diamonds Fanny was wearing. They also patted down Béla's coat and took away his gold coins. They did leave little Rita alone and so the family was able to leave with her small diamonds. Later, when they arrived in Israel, they would also find no one was much interested in buying Romanian art.

Despite all their problems, Béla remained euphoric as the Transylvania released three deep reverberating blasts from its steam horn, and the overloaded passenger ship ponderously pushed off from the dock, out into the Black Sea. It was Béla's second voyage to try and find a better life, and he silently prayed to a God he didn't really believe in that this time his escape would be successful.

Fanny was quiet, pensive, lost in her own thoughts as she held tightly onto her little girl's hand. Rita was excited. For her, everything was a great adventure and she giggled as she waved to the strangers on the shore as if she knew them all, and she scrunched up her shoulders in mock terror each time the captain let loose another blast from the ship's horn.

Béla tried to comfort his young wife. "We're the lucky ones," he said. "At least we have our own cabin," he remarked as he pointed toward the poor unfortunates who would be forced to make the voyage living and sleeping on the cold wet decks.

But Fanny did not feel particularly fortunate. She was deeply anxious about her separation from her family back in Fălticeni. When she made a last trip with Rita to bid her family good-bye, she learned that they had also put in applications to emigrate to Israel, but were denied permission to leave. As the ship headed out into the choppy waters, Fanny was apprehensive about a future she suspected would not be as easy or as bountiful as Béla insisted it would be.

Chapter Seven: Tent City

Der mentsh trakht un got lakht.
Man plans and God laughs.
—Bernstein, Jüdische Sprichwörter und Redensarten.

The Romanian ship *Transylvania* was originally built in 1938 by Burmeister and Wain, shipbuilders in Copenhagen, Denmark, as a passenger cruise ship intended to sail the Black Sea and the Mediterranean, loaded with 80-first, 100-second, and 230-third class passengers on holidays. However, once World War II broke out and Romanian shipping was regularly bombed by the Soviet navy and air forces, the owners kept the ship docked quietly in a port in Istanbul, Turkey, until the war ended.

After the war, it became obvious that there was a lot of money to be made providing passage for Jews wishing to make the over 1,000-mile journey from the port city of Constanța, Romania—through the Black Sea, then the Bosporus Strait, then the Sea of Marmara, then the Dardanelles Channel, then the Aegean Sea, and then the Mediterranean Sea—southeast, to the port of Haifa in Israel. The owners were more than happy to double the normal fare and pack the ship with 1,300 Jews for the week-long trip, twice a month, month after month, regular as clockwork, on a boat built to carry 410.

Béla, Fanny and Rita were very fortunate to have their small cabin, but even so, the voyage through rough seas on a boat carrying three times more people than it was designed to carry was very unpleasant. Dining halls served basic meals of bread, weak tea, thin soup, bad cheese and stale vegetables. Toilets were backed up. The decks were so crowded, little Rita was in constant danger of being accidently tumbled overboard. As a result, Fanny and Rita spent much of the voyage in their cramped, poorly-ventilated cabin, sea-sick and miserable.

Béla refused to be sick. He wandered around the *Transylvania,* talking to anyone he could engage in conversation, trying to get information about what their situation would be once they reached Eretz Israel. Unfortunately, his conversations ended up revealing the same little-bit-of-this, little-bit-of-that stories, mixing partial information with individual made-up expectations that he had heard in the emigration line in Bucharest: everything was prepared for the new arrivals, nothing was prepared or organized and the country was in total chaos; business would be good, business would be bad; there were plenty of jobs, there were no jobs; it was chilly and dry, it was hot and rainy; people were living in fabulous new houses, people were sleeping in the streets; the Arabs would kill you, the Arabs would help you. And so it went. Still, there was general optimism that whatever their sacrifices, they were the price to pay for their glorious new life in the Holy Land where both the good and the bad would be the results of their own Jewishness, not an overlord's anti-Semitism.

In reality, the experience that the eternally-enthusiastic Béla had hoped for upon arriving in Haifa, to begin a new life in the land of Moses—described in the Bible as flowing with milk and honey—turned out not to be encouraging. For one thing, immediately upon disembarking from the *Transylvania*, he and his family were faced with the chaos of the reception centers where thousands of Jews from scores of countries, speaking a Babel of languages, were being processed into a brand new country with little or no established bureaucratic, economic or societal infrastructures.

Béla was carrying both suitcases. Fanny was carrying Rita as they waited in long queues under the warm sun, in multiple layers of dark and heavy European clothes totally inappropriate for the Israeli weather. Fanny and Rita were already sick from their voyage and getting sicker as they inhaled the stench of diesel fuel, the sweat from thousands of bodies, and the odors of urine and feces wafting from the inadequate banks of toilettes provided for the bedraggled immigrants.

Béla fought to raise their flagging spirits and even to boost his own, refusing to allow his fatigue and frustration to show on his face. He smiled for Fanny. He joked with Rita and tousled her thick curly hair.

"Only one hundred more waiting lines," he joked.

"That's not funny," groused Fanny. "I'm not sure I can even make it through this one."

"When will we be home, *Tata* (Daddy)?" Rita begged. "I am so tired. I am so hot."

"It won't be long," Béla answered gamely.

But it was a long time. Even as they moved closer to the immigration shelter itself—really, just a long arcade with a canvas roof to block out the hot sun and, mercifully, open on all sides to allow the meager breezes to blow through—Béla could hear the barked questions from the overworked Israeli immigration officials and the confused answers from bewildered new arrivals that only meant more delays for the others in line, and more waiting. Always waiting.

"I'm hungry, Mama" whined Rita, holding more tightly to Fanny's hand and pulling at her. Fanny looked toward Béla.

"It won't be long," repeated Béla, the phrase becoming his mantra.

"But I'm hungry," wailed Rita, adopting her own mantra—the mantra of children everywhere forced to endure long lines and continual discomfort.

Fanny looked around and saw a small group gathered near a water spigot. She carried Rita to the spigot where she and Rita were able to at least drink cool water.

Finally, it was Béla's turn to be processed.

Name? Wife's name? Child's name? Country of origin? Emigration papers from Romania? Status? Were you or your immediate family in the camps? No, I mean your present family? Your wife? Béla unintentionally hesitated for a moment. Your child? So you were citizens of Romania? Bucharest? I see. I see. Just a minute. Check these papers. Check these forms. Check these lists. Check those lists. Um. I see. Okay. Well, Family Izsák, *Bruchim HaBayim!* (Welcome to Israel). Here's your temporary pass. Get in that line over there, and you will be taken to Absorption Center Three.

"That's where we'll live?" asked Béla.

"No, no. That's where you'll stay for a week or so while you and your family are processed."

"Processed? To where?"

"I don't know."

"Please," said Béla, "if possible, I would like to be placed in the coldest part of Israel."

For a moment, the man just stared at Béla. Then he shook his head in amazement. "The cold part?"

"Yes, so I can practice my trade. As a furrier."

The man couldn't contain himself any longer as he started to chuckle. "My friend," he said, "There are no really cold parts to our beautiful land." Then he laughed even harder. "And you best hope you're not sent up to the northern border. Forget furs! They're so poor up there, one is lucky to have a wool sweater."

Béla was a little embarrassed by his ignorance, but he smiled anyway in an attempt to be amiable. Then, Béla and Fanny and Rita trudged over to the macadam two-lane road to wait in another line for a bus that had seen better days—the tan paint was faded almost white, the windows were gone, the engine smoked, the transmission clattered. Eventually they arrived at a field where there were a series of recently constructed barracks—the wooden plank walls painted drab green, and the grounds, a mixture of sand and dirt and gravel, with the occasional tiny tree or flowering shrub planted in a futile attempt to brighten up the institutional, temporary nature of the place.

Their days were spent filling out forms, reading forms, sitting during boring and not very informative orientation sessions, or gossiping with the other families. Everyone in the center experienced the same stressful mixture of anticipation and ignorance.

Béla could usually be found with a group of Romanian and Hungarian men sitting on the steps outside the meeting hall, smoking cigarettes, gesticulating, arguing, laughing. Suddenly, some of the younger men would be shouting and yelling, then running around scuffling and shoving each other like little boys on the schoolyard, then just as suddenly they would drop back onto the ground, sitting or lying, waiting, waiting for something to happen. Sometimes they kicked around an old soccer ball. Sometimes they did push-ups or jumping jacks. Most of the time they did nothing at all.

The women sat in small groups of twos and threes while their children ran and played. Fanny was cautious, withdrawn, not overly friendly with the other women. She read the information sheets carefully, studied the handouts concerning medical aid and hygienic advice. She scoured through the family's meager belongings, taking inventory of what little remained. She badgered the center's authorities concerning what supplies would be forthcoming and when they would arrive. She tried to plan ahead, but since that was impossible, mostly she worried, concerned about her fate and the fate of her family.

Rita found a playmate, a light brown, very thin Yemeni girl dressed in a vivid flower-patterned smock. She had large, deep oval eyes and a big smile. They approached each other timidly at first. They had no common language other than the gestures and expressions children use for their effective juvenile telepathy.

They noticed each other as they were leaving the dining hall. The Yemeni had her hand tightly wrapped around a scrap of golden yellow fabric that attracted Rita's attention. Rita smiled. The girl smiled back. Rita cocked her head toward the girl's hand. The little girl slowly, tentatively, held out the piece of fabric toward Rita. Strings had been tied to create a tiny head and miniature arms and legs. A face had been inked onto the head. A very small doll. The girl's treasure.

Rita knew better than to reach for the doll. Instead, she leaned in and examined the yellow handmade puppet. For all of its utter simplicity, the doll represented everything Rita had lost. The other girl had her meager treasure; Rita had nothing.

The Yemeni girl sensed Rita's sadness. She pushed her hand forward, indicating that Rita could hold the simple cloth. Rita understood the girl's gesture, touched the golden doll and held it to her heart. The two girls exchanged smiles and nods. Soon they were playing together in the shade next to the dining hall, building doll houses out of dirt, sand and rocks, placing the tiny puppet in different rooms and walking her down imaginary streets. Rita never learned the other girl's name and never saw her again after that day's play.

Unbeknown to Béla and Fanny, the Israeli government had run out of places to house the hundreds of thousands of newcomers streaming into the country. The earliest waves of immigrants from the 1880s were often youthful, idealistic Jews from Russia and Poland who arrived in Palestine to connect to the land. These early pioneers cultivated the land and developed communal living in agricultural kibbutzim. After, came the *Aliyah Aleph*, the relatively controlled immigration during the years preceding WWII and during the war itself. Then, in the three years after Israel declared independence in 1948, over 700,000 Jews had entered Israel, more than 118,000 from Romania alone. These were in addition to the hundreds of thousands who had entered Palestine legally and illegally during what was called the *Aliyah Bet* after the end of WWII when Palestine was still under British mandate. Of course, Israel wanted this massive immigration. Indeed, the future of the country depended on it. But the results sometimes felt like the old maxim, "Be careful what you wish for."

By the late 1940s, Israel had run out of accommodations in her cities, small towns or the kibbutzim to house new arrivals. It was unthinkable to place any limits on immigration, so it was decided to create *Ma'abarot*—temporary communities that were initially made up of small single-family tin houses—throughout the country to house immigrants. Soon, these tin cities were also filled to capacity and the supply of tin was needed for more important uses, among them the ongoing conflicts with the Arab countries that surrounded Israel. So the next step was to construct tent towns that were often placed on the outskirts of large cities.

While all of the *Ma'abarot* housing units were intended to be temporary, and most of the communities had disappeared by the mid-1950s, the conditions in these *Ma'abarot* were very harsh. In some communities it had been reported that there were 350 people to each shower and in others, 56 to each toilet. What's more, although the earliest immigrants from the official Displaced Persons camps in Eastern Europe and Cyprus were granted financial assistance by the Israeli Jewish Agency, later immigrants placed in the *Ma'abarot* were pretty much left on their own to fend for themselves.

On the following day after Rita had finally made a new friend, the Izsáks were summoned and told they would be moved to their designated home. Rita was upset. She tried to find the Yemeni girl to tell her she was leaving, but she could not find her and Béla and Fanny told Rita there wasn't time to search the whole center.

"There will be new friends in your new home," said Fanny

"I don't want a new home," pouted Rita.

"Life can be mean," said Béla.

"No. You're mean," said Rita, and she plopped herself down on one of the suitcases and she wouldn't move.

Actually, there would have been time for Rita to seek her friend. After being summoned, the Izsáks hurried and then waited. Another line in the hot sun.

Finally, a convoy of motley trucks arrived. Some were reconditioned troop transports and some were simply dilapidated delivery vans. All of them burned oil, belched acrid smoke and rattled and shook precariously as they drove onto the center's grounds. The Izsáks were loaded onto the trucks along with their state-issued military cots, mattresses, a two-burner gas range, a kerosene lamp and a few pots and dishes to be taken to their *Ma'abara* (tent) which they had been told was on the outskirts of Rehovot, a town in the center of the country, a fact that had no meaning to them at that point in time.

Rita was still pouting as Béla lifted her into the back of one of the transports. "I'm hungry, *Tata*," she said.

"We'll be there soon," said Béla, although he should have known by then that nothing happened quickly in the new Israel. The trucks jumped and rattled over the bumpy, rutted dirt and gravel roads. Dust billowed up behind them and sometimes blew inside their truck, covering them with a thin film of dark brown dirt that looked like blood when it mixed with the moisture of their sweat and snot from constant sneezing.

Rita said: "I'm tired, Mama." She rested her head on her mother's lap. Fanny rubbed her child's back and Rita, mercifully, fell off to sleep for the remainder of the journey.

It was late in the evening and dark when their convoy arrived at its destination. As Béla jumped down from the back of the truck in eager anticipation, he looked around him and didn't see any houses or streetlights or stores or people other than those emerging from the other trucks. He latched onto the truck driver and asked, "Where are we? Where is our new village?"

The driver, himself tired and annoyed, brushed off Béla's hand and raised his arm in a sweeping gesture. "Here. Here is your home."

Béla peered into the darkness and all he could see were rows and rows of tents. "Tents," he said. "We're to live in tents?"

"Be thankful you have these," said the driver as he began to unload the truck.

Béla lifted an exhausted Fanny and a groggy Rita out of the truck and did his best to put on a brave face. "We're here," he said cheerfully, "ready to begin our next fun adventure."

Fanny was at first too disoriented to say anything. Then she realized where she was. "Tents?" she mumbled to Béla. Then louder, in rising anger, "Tents!"

"They look like fairly large, sturdy tents," said Béla. Fanny had no response.

As they approached their assigned shelter and pulled back the flap to enter, Fanny exclaimed, horrified when she saw the tall grass and weeds, "There's no floor!"

While workers dumped cots and mattresses, the cook stove and a few pots, pans and dishes into the weeds and left, Béla tried to quickly organize the tent. He immediately realized that one cot and mattress were missing. He ran after the workers who were loading themselves back onto the trucks. "Wait," he cried, "Wait. We're missing one cot and one mattress." But the workers wanted to get to their own homes and the trucks roared off, leaving Béla staring into the darkness.

As he entered his family's tent, he heard his little Rita tell Fanny: "This is not a home, Mama."

It was her daughter's simple declaration that finally broke down Fanny's stoic resolve. She melted into tears and collapsed onto her lumpy mattress. Rita, upset by her mother's crying, also began to cry and she climbed into bed and curled up next to her mother. Even Béla felt his chest heave and he was wracked with silent sobbing as he lifted the tiny gas range and moved it into the corner of their tent. Then he turned out the kerosene lamp while the three of them wept in the dark on the rough edge of despair.

Chapter Eight: Horses and Ice Blocks

In a sheynem epl gefint men a mol a vorem.
In a beautiful apple you sometimes find a worm.
—Stutchkoff, Der Oytser fun der Yidisher Shprakh.

On the following morning, neighbors who had arrived a few weeks before and who were also from Romania and somewhat "acclimated," greeted Béla and Fanny, brewed hot coffee for them, and then oriented them to the communal baths and communal toilets on the edge of tent city.

In many ways, the Izsáks were fortunate to be placed on the outskirts of Rehovot, rather than in the more remote countryside. Originally, it was founded as the *moshava* of Rehovot (in a *moshava*, as opposed to a commune like a *kibbutz*, all the land and property are privately owned) on land that was under the control of the Ottoman Empire at the time. The land was purchased from Arab settlers by the Menuha Venahala society of Warsaw, an organization that raised funds for Jewish settlement in Eretz Israel.

At that time, in the 1880s, the region was an uncultivated wasteland. The new settlers dug deep wells, planted Eucalyptus trees to drain the swampy land and planted vineyards and citrus groves, so by the time Béla and Fanny arrived, Rehovot was no longer inhospitable. It was a well-established town with wide roads, large leafy trees and estates owned by orchard growers—the descendants of those first pioneers who arrived from Poland and Russia.

The city of Rehovot also had the advantage of being strategically placed on the route connecting Tel Aviv to Jerusalem. When Béla and Fanny arrived in Rehovot, and for many years later, the long *Rehov HaRashi* (Main Street), running west to east, mirrored the ethnic and social strata of the population. At the immediate edge of town, entering the city from the direction of Tel Aviv, were the oases of two research institutions (the Weizmann Institute of Science and the Agricultural Institute) and neighborhoods populated mostly with relatively affluent Ashkenazi Jews. From there, Main Street continued toward the bustling center of town, past an imposing relic (the police station) from the period of the colonial occupation of Palestine by the British, to a major intersection (with *Rehov Yaakov*), where turning in one direction would lead to the central bus terminal (*Tahana Merckazit*) and a movie theater (*Kolnoa Beit HaPoalim*), while turning in the opposite direction would lead to the public school (*Ganon* and *Beit Sefer Amami*), to the public library (*Sifriat Ahad Haam*), and to another movie theater (*Kolnoa Ahad Haam*), all these institutions adjacent to one another. At the eastern edge of town, on the way out toward Jerusalem, were the poorest neighborhoods populated largely by Sephardic Jews from Yemen.

The Weizmann Institute was founded by the prominent European Zionist, eminent biochemist and first President of Israel, Chaim Weizmann, who lived on the grounds in his large house even while he was president of the country. The fortunes of the Izsáks would later come to be tied to the Institute, as the trajectory of their lives ultimately advanced from the eastern part to the western part of town, but not in the linear path Béla hoped that it would.

For all of the advantages of being near a major city, there remained enormous obstacles for the new immigrants living in the tents of the Rehovot *Ma'abarot*. Chief among them was the fact that the only way to get out of living in the tent city was to save enough money to rent an apartment, but there was virtually no work for the thousands living in the *Ma'abarot*, so Béla's first 'job' was actually installing new tents for the ever-growing community of immigrants arriving from the Diaspora. For this work, he was paid virtually nothing—barely enough to buy food to feed his family.

And his family was growing. Fanny's brother, Aşu, the same brother who had originally discouraged Fanny from marrying Béla, was the only other member of Fanny's family to be granted permission to leave Romania in 1951. The rest of the family, on both Béla's and Fanny's sides, would have to wait almost fifteen years longer to finally get out of Romania and be reunited in Israel. When Aşu arrived in Haifa, Béla met him as he disembarked from the *Transylvania*. Béla presented him with a few precious bananas that Fanny had managed to gather as a welcoming present, but Aşu, who had never before seen a banana, grabbed one and bit into it without peeling it, as if it were an apple or a peach.

"Ugh, these are terrible," said Aşu as he spit out his mouthful of thick rubbery peel and soft fruit. Then, he impulsively pitched the remainder of the bananas into the Mediterranean, not realizing how valuable they were. As Béla sadly watched the bananas sink below the surface of the sea, he did his best to hold back his temper and remain in a jovial mood as the two headed back to Rehovot.

When they arrived at Béla's tent home, Aşu was astonished to see the thick pole in the center that held up the tent. He asked, "What is this, a circus?" Béla again held his temper while Fanny hugged her brother, overjoyed to see him, laughed and said, "Sometimes, Așu, I do think this is a circus." In many ways it was, because Așu also began living in the tent with Béla, Fanny and Rita, sleeping on his own military cot. They were soon joined by a large orange cat that Rita enticed into staying with them when she offered the feral animal a small dish of milk, after the beast slipped in under the flap one morning early. With the addition of the wild cat, they truly were living life under the big top.

Așu joined the household just as Béla and Fanny were trying to mend a deep emotional rift between them following an abortion that Fanny sought without informing Béla. Béla was furious when he found out about this, rejecting Fanny's explanations that, "The tent is not a place to bring up another child," and "Our life is already stressed by so much hardship." Béla's attitude was that, "A sibling for Rita would have been fine, regardless of our circumstances." Fanny was always the level-headed realist; Béla always was the romantic dreamer.

Even with Așu working, there was never enough money, so Fanny found backbreaking work picking oranges. She was young, she worked hard and soon she graduated to the more coveted position of sorting oranges. Then she advanced further to packaging oranges for export. And when oranges were not in season, Fanny found work in a factory that manufactured tablecloths, where her job was to fold the cloths along precise sharp lines. All day she was tirelessly folding one tablecloth after another, after another. Her work life was terrible, but each advancement, although far from the sophisticated, luxurious life she had lived in Bucharest, gave her a small sense of accomplishment and encouraged her to focus on building a future.

Rita had the easiest time of it, because, after all, living in a tent, surrounded by families from all over Europe, North Africa and the Middle East, most of them with children whose parents were struggling and had little time for strict supervision of their little ones, and the children therefore running and playing wild and free, was a carefree life with unexpected adventures filling each day. Moreover, Rita was an outgoing child, easy to laugh, open to new experiences, eager to make friends.

Rita's two favorite conspirators were an Iraqi girl from Bagdad and a little boy from Esfahan, Iran. None of the three spoke the same language and none of them had yet been in school where they would eventually learn their new common language, Hebrew, but that didn't stop them making forts from small packing boxes abandoned near the supply shed, peeking around the communal baths to catch unwary naked settlers taking showers, or screaming down the aisles between the tents, pretending they were being chased by *golem*—Rita's short legs pumping furiously, the Iraqi girl's blue scarf trailing behind her in the dirt, and the Iranian boy's thick black curls bouncing atop his laughing eyes. Those were good days for the children.

It was the usually optimistic Béla who was having the roughest time. He did eventually find a job outside of the tent city, but it was horribly unpleasant, smelly, dangerous work, standing in the blazing sun atop the estate houses of descendants from the early pioneers, tarring roofs and inhaling the acrid fumes of the smoking pitch. This was not at all the life he had envisioned when he decided to leave Bucharest, and there were times when he complained bitterly, occasionally even wondering if he should have stayed in Romania. Furthermore, he was nearing 40, while Fanny and Așu were still in their early twenties.

"How could life under Communism be worse than this?" he exclaimed one night after dinner.

It was Așu, in touch with relatives back home in Fălticeni, who spoke up. "No, Béla, it's not just Communism. The old ways are returning to the countryside and there are new laws against Jews. Soon there will be big problems for Jews in Bucharest as well, Communists or no Communists."

"But…" Béla began.

Așu Interrupted him. "No, Béla, you made the right decision. Our life back there is over. There's no going back."

"Așu is right," said Fanny as she sat on her cot beneath the tent's kerosene lantern mending another pair of pants Béla had ripped open when he tripped and almost fell off a roof. "Israel is our future." A fierce, determined look crossed her face. "We will make it work."

After that conversation, Béla pulled himself together and started his own business. He had always been an entrepreneur, so he started thinking: Standing on hot rooftops had made him realize how very much Israelis needed refrigeration. Even a cursory examination of the homes in tent city and the poorer homes of Rehovot reminded him that few had electric refrigerators. It was then that he understood how important the business of delivering ice was in this hot dry climate. And that was when he took notice of the ice delivery men who carried large blocks of ice, door to door, in their horse-drawn carts. On the upside, he mused to himself, at least I will get to work with the cold, as I asked for when I first arrived at Haifa. But he was forced to admit that delivering ice was a long way away from the furrier business. On the downside, he quickly realized, he didn't have a delivery cart or a horse.

Buying a cart proved easy enough. Béla understood the mechanics of wheels and axles and the reliability of wood and fastenings and even the condition of leather harnesses. He had knowledge and judgment about these things. He knew absolutely nothing about horses.

He'd heard somewhere that you could tell a horse's age by checking its teeth, so when he visited the horse trader, a bent old Arab, brown and weather-beaten as an old boot, Béla tried to appear knowledgeable by attempting to force open the mouth of the first horse he saw. The horse resisted aggressively and tried to bite Béla.

"Son-of-a-bitch, what do you think you're doing?" shouted the trader.

"Oh," said Béla as he stepped back. "Just trying to figure out how old this one is," Béla mumbled as nonchalantly as he could manage.

The trader laughed. "Fuck you! Keep that up and it's more likely you'll lose a few fingers," the trader growled. "So, why do you need a horse?"

"To pull my ice cart."

The trader tried to steer Béla toward three old swaybacked mares that were tiredly munching from a hay bale. But Béla was not to be fooled. He spotted a strong young stallion, tall in the haunches, well-muscled flanks, snorting and pulsing with energy. "That's a beautiful horse," said Béla.

"Oh, you don't want that one for pulling a cart," said the trader as he spat on the ground. "Come on over here," and he continued toward the mares.

Béla was sure the old man was trying to trick him. "How much for that one?" Béla asked, pointing back toward the stallion.

The trader rolled his eyes and shook his head. "You don't want that one."

"How much?"

The trader named a price. Béla offered half as much, expecting to haggle. The trader chuckled. "Well, okay, you can have him."

Béla was delighted at his good fortune. "What's his name?" asked Béla.

"*Haziz* (Thunderbolt)," replied the old Arab.

"Okay, *Haziz*," Béla smiled. "We'll finish our deliveries twice as fast as the other icemen."

However, instead of finishing twice as fast, it often seemed to take them three times as long. First, there were the struggles of harnessing the aggressive Thunderbolt. Every morning, Béla would brave a long and difficult face-off with this unyielding horse. As soon as Béla approached with the harness, Thunderbolt would kick with his front legs, then rear up on his hind legs, and from that menacing height he would neigh threateningly. When the horse finally landed again on all four legs, Béla would try to reach for the mane to stop him from pulling back, but the horse would again kick and jump, neigh and snort.

"Aha," grumbled Béla, furious and out of breath. "That's what the old Arab was trying to tell me. This horse is no good for pulling a cart." This intimidating, predictable routine would repeat over and over until the horse finally tired. Béla would manage to throw the harness over Thunderbolt's back, connect the harness to the cart, and tighten the reins. And although he would never be tamed, Thunderbolt did eventually make the rounds during the heat of the day, every day, without faltering or refusing to move forward.

But then, every few weeks, Thunderbolt would kick open the door to his stall and flee in a mad dash for freedom, tearing through the neighborhood in the middle of the night, trampling down outhouses, chicken coups, planters and shrubs. Béla was then forced to deal with the wrath of neighbors, and he was often threatened with lawsuits. Sometimes, he even had to take time off from his deliveries to go to court where, with his fragile command of Hebrew, he tried to defend himself and haggle to lower the damages that he was ordered to pay.

As if his horse was not enough trouble, protecting his route from extremely aggressive, ruthless competitors was a full time job in itself. Life in the *Ma'abara* was always a struggle and everyone was trying to get a leg up. Every few days, there were new intruders trying to poach on Béla's territory. Many without a permit. Tempers flared. Harsh words were exchanged. Fists flew. Each evening, Béla arrived home exhausted, back aching, knuckles raw from lifting the heavy, cold blocks of ice or brawling with the other drivers. But at least he owned his own business. At least he was getting ahead.

The days dragged on. Fanny rose up the ranks at the orange processing plant. Rita's mini-gang rampaged through tent city, alternating between annoying and entertaining the other settlers with their charmingly outrageous pranks. Aşu joined the Israeli army and went off to fight the Arab enemies pressing against Israel's borders. His absence gave Fanny and Béla a little more space. In the evening they would stroll through the camp, listening to the hundreds of loud voices calling out in a cacophony of Hebrew, the many dialects of Arabic, Romanian, Russian, Polish, Hungarian and Yiddish. Delicious smells wafted from food stalls selling humus, falafel, sweet *Rahat Al-halkum*, spicy *mici*, corn on the cob and watermelon. Life was slowly improving.

Fanny and Béla particularly looked forward to their evening strolls when the *hamsin* was blowing very hot, very dry desert wind from the Sahara through Egypt into Israel. Daytime during a *hamsin* was brutal. There was not only heat, but there were fine particles of sand that scratched their eyes and scoured their throats. Then at sundown the winds would calm and there would be a cool breeze.

Sometimes the end of the *hamsin* would also bring rain. Those occurrences were truly a blessing because the rains would bring clean, fresh air and wash the gritty dust from the buildings, sweep the sandy streets and moisten the hard baked earth. On one such evening, Fanny and Béla were in an upbeat mood. Béla's fears that he'd made the wrong decision by moving to Israel were fading and Fanny was optimistic that their finances, small as they were, were finally in order. They held hands and shared an affectionate kiss while Rita played on the dirt floor of the tent.

Suddenly, deep-rolling thunder disturbed the calm and bright lightening flashes traced across the nighttime sky. Béla heard the splat, splat as fat raindrops hit the roof of their tent. He hurried to make certain the flaps were lowered and secure while Fanny lifted Rita into her arms and they cuddled on one of the cots to listen to the thunder. Despite the heavy weather outside, Rita felt warm and safe and comforted in her mother's arms as she drifted off to sleep.

Then, in the middle of the night, in the deepest dark, Rita heard her mother and father talking in nervous, worried voices. The winds were howling and violently shuddering the tent's canvas walls. Then she heard a soft splashing sound when Béla's feet hit the ground, and more splashing as he sloshed over to light the kerosene lamp hanging on the center pole. Rita looked over the edge of her cot and saw ankle-deep water swirling across the floor of the tent. Then the sirens, usually activated to warn of an imminent air raid, blared. Rita heard panicked voices from outside screaming and shouting, "Get out, get out! Move to higher ground! Get out!"

Fanny and Béla grabbed a few belongings, but Béla had to carry Rita because the water was rising so quickly that the current was pulling against his calves. They trudged outside into the mud, the pouring rain and gale-force winds, following the other families fleeing the *Ma'abara* and heading toward the center of Rehovot.

The next day the sky was brilliant blue and the air sparkling and clear, but the storm had brought complete devastation to the *Ma'abara*. The waters had carried off the settlers' personal possessions. The meager furniture and the cots were strewn about, covered in mud. The tents had blown over and were collapsed into torn and broken heaps on the slimy ground.

Rita was taken with the other children to be sheltered in the *Beit HaKnesset HaGadol* (Grand Synagogue), where there was warm food, bedding and watchful supervision. Fanny and Béla, along with the other settlers were housed in various schools, sturdier structures that had survived the torrent. But everything was gone. Everything.

When they returned to their vanished *Ma'abara* to view the damage, Fanny's strength broke and she allowed herself to bury her head on Béla's chest and weep. Béla placed an arm around her shoulder while her sobbing beat a ragged rhythm against his own heaving body. And in that moment, although he would continue to fight, continue to hold on to even the thinnest hope, something broke inside him and he would never be able to restore his original vision that Israel was where he wanted to be.

(above) Flooded tent city in the Ma'abara near Rehovot in 1953, with Béla trying to rescue the few family belongings.

(below and next page) Béla in early 1950s, an entrepreneur in Rehovot, Israel, with shabby wagon and lethargic donkey that replaced Thunderbolt, selling ice blocks to a population in a place and a time before refrigerators.

Chapter Nine: Growing Alienation

Nit mit sheltn un nit mit lakhn ken men di velt ibermakhn.
Neither cursing nor laughing can change the world.
—Bernstein, Jüdische Sprichwörter und Redensarten.

Poor Béla. Sometimes it seemed as if every time he made progress forward, he was thrown back into chaos and confusion. How many new lives would he have to pursue before he found what he was looking for? And sometimes he wasn't even sure exactly what he was looking for. But there he stood on the outskirts of Rehovot with a strong-willed wife, a playful daughter, a crazy horse and no place to live, so he at least knew the first thing he needed to look for was a new home.

In some ways, the destruction of the *Ma'abara* was a blessing because it forced Béla and Fanny into the next stage of the Israeli immigrant experience as it happened in the early 1950s. While it was clear that people were not going to live in tin houses or tents for the rest of their lives, it was also true that the infrastructure and the economy of the new state could not possibly absorb the continuing tidal waves of immigration by providing luxury accommodations and graceful living. Everyone had to make do, and what was once unthinkable had to become acceptable and manageable.

Béla and Fanny eventually found an apartment on the grounds of a large old estate owned by a *Sabra* (Israeli-born) widow whose family had settled in Rehovot when it was a dry, vacant field and who, after decades of struggle, had achieved a certain wealth and status. Her name was Madam Traivish and she was tall, strong and defiant, with thick, long, unruly salt-and-pepper hair and a ruddy weather-beaten complexion. She had green eyes and she wore thick, rimless glasses. Unfortunately, her riches had not made her a particularly kind or generous person and her personality was truly *Sabra* in the negative way, since *Sabra* is also the Hebrew word for the prickly pear cactus.

Madam Traivish no longer kept horses, so she had converted her stables into three small apartments. Whether she did so out of a patriotic desire to help absorb her country's immigrants or to increase her personal wealth, no one can say for sure, but her conversions accomplished both goals: They housed immigrant families and they were expensive, given how primitive they were.

The Izsák's apartment was essentially one large room with an attached tiny kitchen and an outhouse in the back yard—a state of affairs neither Fanny nor Béla ever thought they would have to endure again but, nevertheless, was preferable to the communal toilets in the *Ma'abara*. The main room served as both the sleeping quarters for Béla, Fanny, and Rita and as a semi-formal living room during the day. There were no closets, so everything had to be stored in an old armoire Fanny bought in the Rehovot flea market.

The tiny kitchen served as sleeping quarters for Aşu when he returned on leave from the army; also as a make-shift bathing room when a galvanized tin bath was brought into it so the family members could take turns bathing in it; and also as a cozy place for socializing—sitting on Aşu's military cot while Fanny was cooking on the two-burner gas stove that she had salvaged from their tent. There was a small sink that was used for washing the dishes and for washing one's face and hands. The laundry washing and the drying were done in the old fashioned way, by hand with washboard and a tub, outside the apartment, and hanging the wet clothes on clotheslines to dry in the sun. The cot in the kitchen was also the place where, in the evening, Béla dumped the *prutot* (coins) from his meager daily earnings selling ice blocks, and where Fanny would later sit and organize this paltry treasure into batches to pay for the rent, the grocer, the butcher, the fishmonger, the baker, and for their one luxury—movie tickets each Saturday night.

Whenever possible, which was most of the time in Israel's warm climate, the family ate outside at a small table and chairs that were placed on an open patio that the Izsáks shared with another Romanian family that occupied the adjoining rental unit. It was usually pleasant to be outside because the one real benefit of the stable apartments was that they were situated deep at the back of the estate's lot, surrounded by Eucalyptus trees, olive trees, and wild flowers that bordered the edge of the property.

However, yet again trouble was on the horizon. On the very first day after signing the lease, when Béla showed up in the evening with his horse and wagon, Madam Traivish came stomping across the empty field, hair flying in the breeze, glasses bouncing on her nose.

"What is this shit!" she screamed. "I rented the apartment to the nice couple with the little girl. Get the hell out of here and get that goddamn animal and broken-down wagon out of here!"

"But…" stammered Béla.

"You're a jackass! I will not have that beast and that…that…," spittle was actually flying from her trembling lips as she charged toward Béla and Thunderbolt. Thunderbolt, of course, did what Thunderbolt always did when he was threatened. He reared up while still in harness, turning over the wagon and dumping Béla on the ground in front of an astonished Madam Traivish. "Well…," she said.

Béla sheepishly picked himself up and brushed himself off as best he could, but he still felt foolish, covered with sweat and dust from another hard day's work. "It was my wife and her brother who came to sign the lease. This horse and this wagon, Madam, that's how I make my money. That's how I will pay my rent."

Madam Traivish was so shaken she couldn't speak. She turned around and headed back to her house, but thirty meters away she called over her shoulder. "You'll regret this, you Romanian idiot!" Then, she continued on and said no more.

Once they were settled in, Fanny began taking courses at the Weizmann Institute and Rita started to attend elementary school. Tuition for the Weizmann courses was paid by the Israeli government as an incentive for new immigrants to learn valuable skills and upgrade their education. Although Fanny continued to work in the orange processing plant, she loved being at the Institute, so she managed to juggle her homemaking, her work and her education in the same focused and determined way she approached every challenge in her life.

Four of Fanny's classmates at Weizmann became close friends and chose to create a study group with her. They often met in Fanny's home to review their readings and prepare for exams. There, under the shade of a Eucalyptus tree in the courtyard, Fanny would set up a table with chairs and bring out a big jar of cool lemonade and a platter with sweet *kugel* (a baked casserole). She would shoo away the noisy children if they hung too close or tried to snatch a *kugel*. Her classmates brought with them their course books and notebooks and scientific rulers, and they would rely on Fanny to guide the discussions and demonstrate the algorithms for solving problems in algebra, calculus, chemistry, physics, and biology.

Rita was proud of her mother's abilities and anxious, because her own adjustment to school was not so smooth at first. Rita spoke Romanian at home with her parents and spoke the same language with her friends, all of them children from the neighborhood, also immigrants from Romania. She could not understand much of what was said in class when the teacher spoke Hebrew in the midst of the linguistic cacophony that was an Israeli elementary school for the nation's international immigrants. To encourage quicker assimilation, the school strongly inhibited the children from speaking in their native Romanian, Turkish, Arabic, Polish, Yiddish, Ladino or any of dozens of other tongues, and strictly enforced a regime of Hebrew, which intimidated Rita.

Rita rebelled. When Fanny dropped her off at the school gate each morning, Rita would run away after two class periods and go home to play with her cat. Since Fanny and Béla were away at work and the house was locked, Rita would play in the courtyard, discretely so she wouldn't be detected by Madam Traivish, until late afternoon when Fanny returned from work. Neither Fanny nor Béla had any idea that Rita was skipping school.

After several weeks of getting away with this behavior, Rita's teacher summoned both parents to discuss their daughter's delinquencies. Fanny and Béla were unnerved by the news. Then, the teacher admonished them to start speaking Hebrew at home and suggested that Béla should register to take a Hebrew course in order to facilitate and accelerate the learning process since Fanny was already taking courses at the Institute. Béla balked but Fanny immediately initiated Hebrew as the language of communications at home, whether Béla agreed or not. Once she mastered the rudiments of the language, Rita became fond of school and fond of learning.

Even Béla was beginning to enjoy life. Yet, each morning when he wheeled out his wagon and each evening when he returned home, he had to suffer the abuse and threats of Madam Traivish who seemed to thrive on her scorn for Béla and Thunderbolt. Béla did his best to ignore her. He reinforced the shed for the horse who continued to somehow escape every so often—a violation that only escalated the war between Béla and Madam Traivish.

Fanny tried to ignore Béla's feud with the landlady, but she had her own special torment. On a large property owned by another landlord, immediately adjacent to the property of Madam Traivish, the owner had built a large reception hall to rent out for weddings and Bar- or Bat-Mitzva celebrations. The reception hall was only about 50 meters away, behind the apartment that Béla, Fanny, and Rita occupied. Once or twice each week and going late into the night, musical bands played loudly, and a boisterous crowd clapped and sang and danced. On hot days, when the large windows of the reception hall were wide open and the raucous sounds blasted into the apartment, Fanny became restless and agitated.

For Rita and her friends in the neighborhood, the raucous celebrations were a constant source of amusement and entertainment. The children would slip over to the neighboring property, scale the wall of the reception hall to reach the windows, and sit on the ledge with their legs dangling inside. Their bodies swayed with the rhythm of the music and they hummed along with the popular tunes in Russian, Yiddish, Italian, and Hebrew that were playing.

There were other small pleasures for the family as well. In the summers, on the Sabbath—the one-weekend day in Israel—large trucks rumbled through the towns and villages of central Israel, collecting passengers, compressed tightly like sardines in the backs of the trucks, heading for the coastal beaches at *Rishon LeZion* or *Bat-Yam*.

Béla was an excellent swimmer and he loved the sea. Of course, in summer everyone loved the water and the beaches were packed with new immigrants enjoying the one inarguable joy of life in Israel—the Mediterranean Sea. The Izsáks would arrive early and sit in a family group on the sand to eat the hearty breakfast they brought with them from Rehovot: hard-boiled eggs, chunks of feta cheese, slices of tomatoes and red peppers, black olives, dark bread and grapes—plain and tasty staples of the Mediterranean diet that everyone around them ate as well. After a short rest, they would take a dip in the warm water. Then, they would walk barefoot along the shoreline for two kilometers or so to where there were large sand dunes, where they would climb atop the dunes to rest and to tan and to gaze at the calm waters of the deep blue sea. "It's so remote from Gâlgău," Béla would sometimes muse wistfully, reflecting on the contrast with where his life started.

After some time, Béla, Fanny, and Rita would walk back, along the shore, through shallow waves tickling their toes, to where they left their bags. At the Bat-Yam beach there was a prominent rock offshore called *HaSella* (the Rock). The rock and smaller boulders formed a large lagoon, excellent for swimming, and strong swimmers enjoyed crossing the lagoon to climb onto the rock. Béla would sometimes swim across the lagoon carrying Rita on his shoulders, surging through the balmy water under the hot sun, relishing hearing Rita's pearls of laughter and squeals urging him forward.

At noon, the same trucks would return to pick up the same crowds, all of them now sweaty and sticky, legs covered with sand and feet tarred from the oil waste that spilled from tankers moving off-shore in the distance. Back at home, the Izsáks would first wipe off the tar with benzene, then shower, then sit down to eat a late lunch, finishing it off with a sweet watermelon, and Sáring the rind with Thunderbolt who would position himself near the table, delightedly crunching the juicy rind with his strong teeth. A short nap followed to recover from the lethargy that enveloped them after the enjoyable time at the beach, and then the happy family would dress in their best clothes to go to the movies to cap off the weekend day—a tradition that held steadfast for many years during those old days before television.

When summer was over, those beach trips would be replaced by dutiful visits out of town (by taxis, because transportation by public buses was outlawed on the Sabbath) to Fanny's relatives, three elderly, childless couples. One of the couples was Nenea Sami and Tanti Betty who arranged the match-making between Béla and Fanny back in Bucharest. The other couples were a brother and a sister of Nenea Sami—all three of them the siblings of Fanny's mother, Malvina, who alone remained in Romania despite repeated bids to join them in Israel. These kindly old people eagerly awaited the visits from the Izsáks, and were thrilled to prepare the lavish dishes from recipes from the Old Country to host their guests from out-of-town.

In her teens, Rita would often rebel against Béla's stubborn insistence that she continue to join Fanny and Béla on these duty-bound visits to the relatives. She preferred to remain behind to go out with friends to the movies or to parties. Béla always prevailed. The friction between them would sometimes escalate, leading Rita to "punish" Béla with 'the silent treatment,' that Fanny then had to broker between them, to bring their dispute to an end.

On other occasions when Béla, Fanny and Rita did not make the rounds to visit the relatives, they would spend the mornings hiking through the vast, sweetly-fragrant orchard groves that surrounded Rehovot, and then wait impatiently for the evening when they could dress up and go to the movies together.

All the films were foreign movies (American, French, Italian, German), so everyone had to rely on the subtitles to follow the plot. Spy movies, Tarzan movies, romantic comedies, heavy tragedies, thrillers—the genre was of no importance. All movies were an escape and were valued. Few people had the means to spend money on hired help to babysit their kids, so children of all ages joined their parents in the cinema. Going to the movies was a spectacle and the chaotic social event for the entire town.

For Rita and her neighborhood friends there was another way to idly pass time. The front of Madam Traivish's property lay alongside an undulating hilly street (*Rehov Menuha VeNahala*), separated from the street by a low wall with a wide opening for access to the courtyard. The children also took advantage of this layout to entertain themselves after school hours. They would sit atop this wall to watch the goings-on in the street. Military vehicles, trucks or jeeps passed by, sometimes stopping to drop off or pick up uniformed soldiers on leave. Men slowly pedaled bicycles with carefully balanced loads in the front. Women, breathing hard, weighed down by heavy loads of groceries carried in bloated clothes bags. Mothers pushing hard against large baby carriages, and young and old couples walking holding hands and sometimes stealing a kiss or a hug. They saw teenage boys bouncing a soccer ball on their way to a playground, and funeral processions advancing on foot, with men carrying the deceased on a stretcher covered in a dark blue velvet cloth and a large Star of David sewn in gold. These street scenes provided amusement and distraction, abundant fodder for gossip, but also rich stimulation to a child's imagination.

But sometimes the street scene was unpleasant for Rita to watch. The children would still be sitting on the wall when Béla returned home in late afternoon after completing his rounds of delivering ice. He was perched on the bench of the rickety wagon, looking forlorn in his standard work uniform—the iconic Israeli *Tembel* hat, a sleeveless white undershirt, Khaki shorts with the money belt around his waist, and worn-out, dusty shoes. He appeared scrawny and haggard. He was pulling briskly at the reins of the harness to slow the horse trotting down the steeply slopping street and finally into the courtyard. This image of her father embarrassed Rita. Among her school friends who sometimes came over to play, were children whose parents were clean and dignified, prosperous doctors or owners of orchards, looking so different from Béla.

The times when the Izsáks lived in the stables apartment brought another simple enjoyment. They had frequent shared meals and small informal parties with the Romanian neighbors whose rental apartment adjoined the Izsáks. The husband and wife were the same age as Fanny, and because they shared a common background and common struggle to make a new life in Israel, a strong bond of friendship was fused.

After several years there, the two families pooled resources and built an annex with plumbing for an indoor toilet and a water heater and shower for shared use. Although the new facility was outdoors, disconnected from their apartments, and going to the toilet or returning from the shower sometimes required running in the rain or in the chilly air, the new washroom was an enormous improvement over using an outhouse and taking baths in a tiny galvanized tub. Madam Traivish did not put up obstacles to building this annex on her property, but she also didn't offer to contribute any amount to cover the expense.

And so life began to settle into a familiar pattern of ongoing work and simple pleasures. Their brief life of luxury in Bucharest slowly faded into the past. Life in Rehovot blossomed. Hope returned that the family was on a slow but steady trajectory to a better life. Aşu met a pretty Romanian girl. They married. Aşu moved out and there was more room in the apartment. Béla delivered his ice blocks. Fanny worked alternately at the orange processing plant or the tablecloth factory, depending on the season of year, and took her classes at the Weizmann.

One morning, in winter, the day began with dark clouds, a chilly breeze and a heavy drizzle. Béla pulled himself out of bed. Fanny was already up and moving about. She made coffee and cut a slice of bread for Béla's breakfast. Then she put together two egg sandwiches, grapes and an orange for Béla's lunch. Béla sat and drank his coffee, reluctant to go out into the wet, chilly air and begin another day hauling ice. Then he threw on a heavy sweater and a canvas jacket, kissed Fanny on the cheek and headed for the shed.

As he approached the shed, he thought it was odd that Thunderbolt wasn't stomping and whinnying as he usually did, especially when the air was damp and cool. He opened the lock on the shed door and saw Thunderbolt collapsed on the ground. Alarmed, he fell onto the ground himself and felt along the horse's smooth long neck. It was cold. No air passed from Thunderbolt's wide nostrils. Béla placed an ear against the beast's chest and heard no heartbeat. He noticed blood on Thunderbolt's gums and teeth. Then he found blisters on the inside of his lip. The horse's eyes were opaque. There was thick yellow mucus on the ground near the horse's nostrils. Béla was far from expert on the death of horses, but he knew instinctively that Thunderbolt had been poisoned.

Béla was enraged. He stomped across the field to Madam Traivish's house and pounded on the door. No one answered. He kept pounding and screaming, "Murderer! Killer!" But still no one answered. Béla vented his anger for a few more minutes but then he realized no one was going to open the door, and so he gave up.

He turned and stumbled away from the house, heading back toward the shed. After about ten or fifteen meters, he stopped and looked back over his shoulder. He saw Madam Traivish standing in an upstairs window staring down at him. Her wild unkempt hair framed her face. She had not put on her glasses, so her piercing green eyes focused intensely on the yard where Béla stood. Then she slowly lifted her right hand and raised her middle finger. A thin, crooked smile passed across her lips.

Béla reached down and picked up a stone. He hurled it toward the window where Madam Traivish was standing, but the stone was slippery and his hand was wet, so the rock landed ineffectually against the side of Madam Traivish's house.

The drizzle turned to a heavy rain as Béla arrived back at his shed. He avoided the dead horse, placed himself between the shafts of his wagon, lifted the poles and slowly trudged off into the mud and pouring rain.

Fanny and Rita ran from the house. Fanny called to him, "Béla, Béla."

Rita pleaded, "*Tata! Tata!*"

But Béla either didn't hear them or chose to ignore them as he passed through the gate, determined to be his own horse, walk his route and complete his deliveries.

Chapter Ten: The Great Escape

Tsores zaynen far dem mentshn vi zhaver far ayzn.
Troubles are to man what rust is to iron.
—Bernstein, Jüdische Sprichwörter und Redensarten.

Can one sit *shiva* (mourn) for a dead horse? The Israeli Ministry of Religious Services and the Chief Rabbinate would not likely approve. However, once his mother, brother and young wife perished in the Holocaust, Béla never cared much for either the ministry or the rabbi, so he mourned Thunderbolt, as did Rita, for a full seven days, even though the poor beast had caused him no end of grief and turmoil. But after all, once under harness, Thunderbolt had always performed his rounds without complaint or delay, and he had been a loyal companion for Rita.

Madam Traivish's treachery reignited Béla's sense of disappointment in his choice to immigrate to Israel. Yes, the climate was wonderful, although not particularly conducive to success in the furrier business. Yes, the determination of the other immigrants amazed him since many were even more optimistic and hopeful than he was, and the emotional and spiritual freedom from anti-Semitism was as exhilarating as he had imagined it would be. But Béla's personal sense of his worth, even his power as a man, felt threatened and this subtle fear made him more tense and irritable than he had been before he arrived in Israel.

It wasn't the difficult, backbreaking work that bothered him. Béla had always been a hard worker. In fact, he thrived on hard work and he'd always left the management and financial decisions to others. But in Bucharest, Béla had risen from being a poor *schlemiel* (easy mark) from the provinces to becoming a successful businessman with a beautiful young wife and a grand apartment. He had status and respect among his furrier colleagues, clients and friends. In Israel, even after six years, he was still at the bottom of the heap, where even the poorest of his customers on his ice delivery route felt free to scream insults or pummel him over the head with a shoe, as one Moroccan woman had done.

Béla's attacks of self-doubt were reinforced by Fanny's opposite trajectory. She was becoming an educated, sophisticated, confidant young woman with more developed tastes, useful knowledge and higher income potential than her older husband. She had become fluent in Hebrew and refused to speak Yiddish because she felt that language represented the humiliations of the Diaspora. She checked out books from the public library and read novels. A friendly colleague from the Institute had introduced her to classical music and she sought to attend every free concert at the Wix Auditorium on the grounds of the Weizmann Institute and even take Rita with her to Tel Aviv once in a while to hear concerts at the Philharmonic. And she associated with smart, world-class scientists and researchers at the Weizmann Institute. Although Béla admired and respected Fanny's accomplishments, he also resented this new woman and, in many ways, he didn't understand her at all.

In addition, he feared losing the respect of his daughter. Rita had also become fluent in Hebrew and she sometimes giggled when she heard Béla's bungled attempts at the language. She had many friends and was very much a comfortable citizen of the new Israel, in so many of the ways that Béla suspected he would never be. And so, he took to buying his child eccentric and inappropriate presents in an attempt to gain her love and attention.

Rita had started to enjoy learning music on her recorder that was given to her at school in order to interest young students in playing a musical instrument. The recorder only whetted her appetite for a more magnificent instrument, so she began bothering her father to buy her a piano. This was an impossible demand, given the family's circumstances, but Rita continued to beg for one despite her father's refusal and her mother's patient explanations that Rita was asking for something that the family simply couldn't afford and had no room to accommodate in their apartment.

One day, Béla came home with a large package sitting next to him on the bench atop his wagon, now pulled by a tired, old, trouble-free but boring gray mare. Béla had a huge smile on his face as he leapt down and lifted the large wrapped object and carried it over to place in front of Rita. Whatever was inside was almost as large as the child who stood there trying to decide if she should be delighted or frightened. "Well," said Béla grandly, "don't you want to open it?"

Rita began to carefully pull away the brown paper to slowly reveal a mysterious object with a vertical keyboard on one end, a set of bellows in the middle and another vertical panel containing a series of buttons on the other end. The non-musical surfaces of the object were laminated in garish blood red, bright orange and florescent green plastic. Rita was dumfounded by the object. Fanny was overcome with astonishment bordering on antagonism.

"Wha…what is it?" stammered Rita.

"Oh my God," exclaimed Fanny in Hebrew.

"An accordion," said Béla, "Like a mini-piano that you can play by strapping it on in front of you and squeezing the sides together." He enthusiastically picked up the object, strapped it on and began to demonstrate, producing the most unattractive caterwauling sounds imaginable.

Fanny grimaced. "It's horrible."

Rita placed her fingers in her ears. "Yuck!" she screamed.

Béla's smiles turned to frowns. "What's wrong?"

Fanny turned and went inside. "Really, Béla…" she huffed.

Rita followed her mother.

Béla shouted after her, "You said you wanted a piano." When the door was closed he yelled, "Ungrateful child!"

A few months later, not long after Rita had wandered home from school with a small, vagrant, flea-ridden, black-and-white puppy that she'd found along the road and was keen to adopt, Béla brought home a large, black, standard-bred poodle. Béla wanted her to accept his gift instead, but she couldn't work up any enthusiasm for the big poodle. She loved her little motley mongrel that she named *Kushi*. Béla was clearly hurt and resented Rita's rejection of his present, but he held his tongue. The next day he simply gave the handsome poodle away to a complete stranger.

While Béla was going through these torments in Israel, back in Europe, in Béla's original homeland, a rebellion was brewing against the Soviet occupation and domination of the Hungarian People's Republic, formed in the aftermath of the defeat of the Nazis in World War II. The revolt began in the fall of 1956, when thousands marched through the streets of Budapest to demonstrate in front of the Hungarian Parliament in support of a series of demands by a group of students who wanted greater freedom from Soviet control of Hungarian affairs. Government troops fired on the demonstrators, one student was killed. His body was wrapped in a Hungarian flag and held aloft above the crowd. This simple act released a flood of emotion that turned into open defiance that quickly engulfed the entire country.

As the unrest spread and various student and workers groups fought skirmishes with the ÁVH (the State Security Police) and Soviet troops, the rebellion became a true revolution. The government fell. An interim government was appointed that pledged to stage new elections. The fighting, more or less, ended and the country appeared to be heading for a peaceful transition. Then suddenly, things changed. The new government, apparently under intense pressure from Soviet Russia, decided to crush the revolution. A large contingent of Soviet troops and tanks entered Budapest and other key regions of the country. Many Hungarians chose to resist. Roughly 2,500 Hungarians and 750 Soviet troops were killed. Within weeks, the revolution was destroyed.

When it became apparent that the revolution would fail and reprisals would be forthcoming, a flood of refugees fled Hungary, many of them crossing over a narrow wooden bridge that spanned the Einser Canal, about 10km distance from the Austrian village of Andau. This event was memorialized in James Michener's famous account of the Hungarian Revolution, *The Bridge at Andau*. These refugees, around 200,000 in all, were then housed in camps in Eastern Austria: in Eisenstadt near the city of Graz and in Traiskirchen, south of Vienna. Approximately 80,000 of these refugees were eventually granted asylum in the United States and 37,000 in Canada.

Both hard news and rumors of these events in Eastern Europe quickly circulated among the Hungarian and Romanian communities in Israel where many of the émigrés, like Béla and Fanny, had left Eastern Europe after WWII in order to avoid turmoil like that which was taking place in Hungary. The Hungarian Revolution and its brutal suppression confirmed the wisdom and foresight of their emigration, but in Béla's mind, these events also stimulated an incredibly courageous and ingenious, if also incredibly cynical and misguided, plot to overcome his problems in Israel by gaining entry to the United States.

While the details of his scheme percolated in Béla's mind, he continued to experience frustration and disappointment in Rehovot. He proudly brought home paintings that he bought in the flea market only to have Fanny declare that the art was amateurish and garish and she would not hang the paintings in her home.

Meanwhile, Fanny had become friends with Aurika, a beautiful, tall, blond young woman, full of gaiety and energy. Fanny found it was fun to be around Aurika, a former classmate from the Weizmann Institute. Aurika and her equally tall and handsome husband, Moshe, lived in the nearby town of *Nes Tziona* (Miracle of Zion), and they became close friends with the Izsáks. Aurika's husband often gave Rita short rides on his motorcycle and she called him '*Chupchik*' on account of the short tussle sticking from the top of the Basque red beret he was sporting. During the couple's frequent visits, Béla was always included in the fun, but he also felt somewhat alienated and distant from the other friends who were closer in age to Fanny.

Then, *Chupchik* contracted tuberculosis. Since this was before the introduction of streptomycin therapy, he was forced to live in a sanatorium for over a year while he was convalescing. As fate would have it, *Chupchik* fell in love with another patient in the sanatorium and he divorced Aurika to marry the other woman.

Fanny and Aurika remained close friends. In the summer after Aurika's divorce, they decided to go on their vacation together, away from Béla and Rita, to a resort in the north of Israel, where Aurika could regain her confidence and spontaneity after the painful end of her marriage and perhaps even find a new boyfriend.

Barely three days into their vacation, Béla showed up at the resort where he found Fanny and Aurika cavorting in the swimming pool with other new friends, among them a few athletic young men. Béla was overcome with jealous rage although the pool play appeared entirely innocent. Béla shouted at Fanny to get out of the pool. Fanny refused.

"Rita and I are sick," said Béla.

"You look well enough to me," retorted Fanny.

"You are a wife and a mother. You have no right to act like this!"

"Like what?" said Fanny. "We're just having fun. You might try it sometimes," she added petulantly.

Her attitude only fueled Béla's anger. "You must return home right now," demanded Béla, waving his hands in the air, his voice rising and insistent. He was creating a terrible scene that was becoming embarrassing for everyone.

Fanny was angry as well, but she quickly realized that the only way she could defuse the situation and allow Aurika to enjoy the remainder of her vacation was to accede to Béla's demands and return home. But she did not do so gently or quietly, and relations between the two of them when they returned to Rehovot were frosty at best.

Rita picked up on the growing tension in the family and she decided that her father was upset because she refused to play her accordion, so in order to make him happy, she picked up the instrument and fiddled with the keys. Gradually, she was able to teach herself a few tunes that she heard on the radio and play them for Béla. Béla could not have been happier as he sang alongside her to *La Donna Mobile*, *Hazam Hazam*, *Tumbalalaika*, *Havah Nagila*, *The Blue Danube* and other tired old standards. As a result, the strategy worked for a while and Béla appeared to relax and enjoy day-to-day life with his family. However, Rita's original objections to the accordion's size and bulkiness and the unladylike posture that was required to play it, made her lose interest again, and she tired of playing only to appease her father.

Meanwhile, Béla's secret obsession with his escape plan grew inside his fertile mind like an explosion of spring flowers on the Negev desert after a heavy rainfall. He listened carefully to every report on the radio about the Hungarian refugees in Austria. He spoke with all his Eastern European friends about any news they had heard from the camps. He gathered up maps and hid them in the shed where he stabled his old docile horse. Late at night he studied the maps and considered the many different ways he could get to Austria and which of those ways was the most likely to succeed. He travelled to Tel Aviv and obtained an Israeli passport, visas and other documents he thought he might need. Every day, he skimmed off a portion of the money he made on his ice route before he left the proceeds for Fanny to count and divvy up for the household expenses. When she noticed the lesser amounts, he complained that his business was shrinking as electricity spread and people had enough money to buy small refrigerators. He waited. He plotted. And he was tortured with guilt and indecision.

It is impossible to know the alternative course of events that might have happened had not Madam Traivish started up again about Béla's horse and delivery wagon. This time her abuse centered on the condition of the new horse—its age, its ragged coat, its swayback appearance, its foul manure droppings as the horse, in some deeply instinctual pique, insisted on depositing near the flower beds just as the wagon passed by Madam Traivish's house.

Béla often saw her standing on her balcony staring at him through her thick spectacles, her wild hair blowing in the wind. As her anger increased, she took to hurling insults again through an open window about Béla's 'fucking ugly beast' and 'flea-bitten nag'. Béla hung his head down low in the humble posture of the defeated and ignored her. Still she persecuted him.

One night, as Béla approached his shed to study his maps, he heard a noise at the back of the shed, and as he went to investigate, he caught a glimpse of Madam Traivish scurrying back toward her house. He entered the shed and saw that a mash of stewed carrots had been left in a pail and the old mare was sniffing the evil brew that she decided was a delicacy. Béla grabbed the pail and managed to get it out of the shed before the horse ate anything. But, Béla thought, so what? This will just continue until she kills the new horse as well.

That morning, before the sun rose, when Béla left on his wagon to service his route, he brought along an old leather satchel filled with his maps, his money, his documents, two changes of clothes and his heavy jacket. Once past the gates of the compound's courtyard, he unharnessed the horse, swatted her on the behind and set her free. Then he abandoned his wagon by the side of the road and walked toward the center of town, hitching a ride to Tel Aviv with a truck driver carrying melons. Then he hitched another ride on a truck carrying tomatoes to the port at Haifa.

"Taking a trip?" the driver asked, noticing Béla's bag.

Béla only nodded. He didn't feel like talking.

"Will you be gone a long time?"

Again Béla only nodded.

The driver realized that, unlike most Israelis, Béla didn't want to talk, so he left his passenger alone on the long bumpy ride, and when they reached Haifa, Béla jumped down from the cab.

"*Beh-Hatzlaha* (Good luck)," shouted the driver.

But Béla didn't even bother to nod as he lowered his head and with a heavy heart headed for the docks.

Chapter Eleven: Italian Episode

Keyner veys nit vemen der shukh kvetsht, nor der vos geyt in im.
No one knows whose shoe pinches except the person who walks in it.
—Bernstein, Jüdische Sprichwörter und Redensarten.

Béla studied a number of different routes to get from Israel to Austria, but, since Israel was surrounded on three sides by hostile Arab neighbors, and all the countries north of Greece were behind the Soviet Iron Curtain, there was really only one way for Béla to travel—by ship from Haifa to Naples, then by foot, bus or rail through Italy, and then over the Alps into the Corinthian region of Austria, and from there to the smaller refugee camp at Eisenstadt near Graz that seemed closer and perhaps more manageable than the larger camp at Traiskirchen outside Vienna.

Once he was near the Eisenstadt camp, Béla planned to slip into, not out of, the camp, mingle with Hungarian refugees from the failed revolution, present himself as also being a Hungarian political refugee and appeal for asylum in the United States, or if that could not be arranged, for asylum in Canada. He chose not to ponder the basic dishonesty of his scheme, reasoning that he was, after all, Hungarian and a refugee, albeit from another conflict, and if he had been in Hungary in October of 1956, he would have, undoubtedly, sided with the Freedom Fighters.

His rationalization for abandoning his family was equally tenuous: why involve them in the scheme? When he was granted asylum, he would send for Fanny and Rita and the whole family could relocate in the United States. If he was lost at sea or waylaid on his journey through Italy, well, better his family simply think he had disappeared and they could go on with their lives. They would be better off without him anyway. Fanny could find a new, younger husband, and Rita would have a father she could be proud of rather than a grumpy old man who shamed her each time she saw him delivering ice blocks from a rickety wagon.

His excuse for giving up Israel, the struggling new nation that had accepted him without question and provided him with sanctuary from the evils of anti-Semitism and possible death, was that he was too old and set in his ways to succeed in the brash, dynamic Israel and he would always feel like a stranger in his own homeland.

So, paradoxically, filled with both self-pity and renewed hope and optimism, in February, 1957, Béla booked passage on the *Aliya*, an aging, rust bucket that was bound for Halifax, Nova Scotia, Canada, and then on to New York City, but he only had an Italian visa and no visa for the US or Canada, so Béla could only remain on board until the *Aliya* stopped in Naples, before continuing to Marseilles, France, and the Atlantic Ocean.

The *Aliya* was originally the former Norwegian liner *Bergensfjord*, one of the ships the newly-formed Israeli passenger service Zim purchased after independence, to legally bring European Jews to Israel. Then, in 1953, she was renamed *Jerusalem* and put in transatlantic service on a route from Israel to Europe to North America and back, still primarily carrying Jews who wished to immigrate to Israel. Starting in 1954, thirty-five new ships were built in West Germany under a reparations agreement for lost property taken from Jews persecuted by the Nazis. Zim received the first new ship in late 1954, which they then also named *Jerusalem*, so the older *Jerusalem* was renamed again, *Aliya*, and kept in service for a few more years only to be sold as scrap in 1959.

Béla took one look at the *Aliya* wallowing in the harbor at Haifa and almost decided to change his mind about sailing on her, but she was the only ship he could afford, so he set sail for Naples in a cramped, lowest-class steerage cabin the following day. Thankfully, weather conditions were favorable and Béla was pleasantly surprised when the *Aliya* made landfall in Italy after four days at sea with no serious problems, except for the fetid odors in the tiny cabin room that forced him outside and on-deck in the crisp, cool air for most of the voyage.

As the *Aliya* entered the stunning Bay of Naples with the charming vista of the city spread out along the hillsides and the imposing Mt. Vesuvius in the background, Béla's spirits soared. He disembarked into the bustling port and emerged from passport control with no complications, bristling with excitement to be in the middle of one of the oldest and largest cities on the Mediterranean.

However, the Naples of the mid-1950s was not the Naples of earlier times. While Naples and its environs was still home to the Bourbon Palace of Caserta—the largest 18th century palace in Europe, and to more archeologically significant castles and churches and museums than even Rome possessed, as well as the ancient ruins of Pompeii and Herculaneum, Naples was also the most bombed Italian city during WWII, suffering punishing aerial attacks from combined British and American forces that killed 25,000 people and flattened important historical landmarks such as the Church of Santa Chiara. Furthermore, Naples had fallen under the influence of the Camorra organized crime families, better known as the Mafia, which managed to choke off the significant redevelopment of infrastructure and services.

Naples ultimately held little attraction for Béla beyond being his introduction back into Europe and, after an uncomfortable overnight sleeping on a bench in the *Stazioni di Napoli Centrale* above the *Piazza Garibaldi*, Béla was able to purchase a cheap, third-class rail ticket—no guaranteed seating—on the early morning train to Rome. He was continuously jostled and bumped and thrown about standing in the jam-packed, smoke-filled passenger car on the twelve-hour ride to Rome. The Italian fascist dictator, Benito Mussolini, may have famously succeeded in making the trains run on time, but the post-WWII Italian trains had reverted to their previous habits and were notoriously slow.

During the journey, Béla found himself making occasional eye contact with a woman of a certain age, mature, attractive, and obviously travelling alone. She had large, sad brown eyes and full lips set in an oval face framed by cascades of thick, black hair. There was a small scar at the base of her chin on the left side of her otherwise smooth, olive-skinned complexion. She wore a black, below-the-knee dress printed with a pattern of small yellow flowers, and a plain, brown, cloth jacket left unbuttoned to reveal the décolletage of her dress and thus her ample bosom. She was short, but stood erect, and somehow able to gracefully maintain her balance in the lurching, shifting rail car.

When the train from Naples finally arrived at the newly completed *Stazioni Termini*—the 1950s modernist, monumental building across the street from the impressive ancient Baths of Diocletian and fronting on the rather uninteresting *Piazzale dei Cinquecento* in the center of Rome, it was early evening and the city was bathed in the romantic golden light of the setting sun.

Béla was hungry, so he stopped at one of the food stands in the plaza, ordered a panini stuffed with sausage and topped with mozzarella and tomato sauce, and a beer. Then he sat under an olive tree to eat and drink and rest, before setting out to find a place to spend the night. As he was finishing his sandwich, the woman from the train also stopped at the food cart. When she saw Béla, she again made eye contact, and Béla nodded, acknowledging that he recognized her. When she received her food, she walked over to the olive tree and sat down next to an astonished, but delighted, Béla and greeted him in Italian, "*Buona sera, signore.*"

He responded in Romanian, "*Bună seara, doamnă,*" so they understood each other's Latin-based greetings, but they both also realized further discussion might be difficult.

Béla drank his beer in silence, trying to decide if he should attempt to speak further with her and, if so, what he could say. The woman ate her food, also in silence. Then Béla finally said, "*Numele meu este Béla Izsák, doamnă.*"

The woman understood. She smiled and answered, "*E il mio nome è Celia, signore, Celia Grillo,*" which Béla understood as well.

Once they crossed that barrier of nervousness, their communication progressed in a torrent of Romanian and Italian, accompanied by common Latin cultural hand-waving, shoulder shrugs, head feints and eye rolls. Before long, they were fast friends. Later, as they walked arm in arm along the *Via del Corso*, searching for the Trevi Fountain, they became close acquaintances. Later that night, in a dingy room in the aptly-named, but exceedingly shabby, *Pensione del Diavolo*, off the *Piazza del Oratorio*, they became intimate lovers.

This Roman interlude was not anticipated in Béla's plans. One part of him, the serious, hardworking, conscientious Béla, was determined that he neither had the money nor the time to be sightseeing and tom catting in the Eternal City. Another part, the gregarious, romantic, self-centered Béla, was content to set aside, for the moment, his goal of reaching the refugee camp at Eisenstadt and experience the sort of unencumbered joy he had not felt since those long-ago days when he arrived in Bucharest from Transylvania and everything had seemed forever possible.

And so, Béla spent two weeks in Rome, absorbing the beauty, even in winter, of the broad boulevards, the ancient Roman fountains and the Renaissance fountains and the Baroque fountains and the cobblestone pavements, and Béla grew stronger from Celia's touch. His self-confidence returned. He was no longer despondent. He was re-armed with boundless optimism and his old mantra—*Don't lose hope*—reappeared in his thoughts and his dreams.

As a result, Béla was relatively carefree when, on the fifteenth day, knowing it was time to go and Sáring a few last kisses and a passionate embrace with Celia, he left Rome, hitchhiking along the highway north toward Florence, because he no longer had enough money to buy even a third-class train ticket. He rode on hay bales in the open beds of smoking diesel lorries, with a large shaggy dog on the back seat of a miniscule Fiat and, for a brief 20-kilometer stretch, in the soft leather comfort of a Dauphine sedan. Even though it was very cold at night, he slept in the wheat fields off the side of the road, ate bread and cheese, drank stagnant pond water that made him sick, but he kept moving.

Outside Florence, he bummed a ride with a family—mother, father and a little daughter—which made him nostalgic for Fanny and Rita. The family dropped him off just south of Bologna, where he had a three-hour wait before a truck filled with crates of squawking chickens stopped and the driver let him sit up-front, all the way to Venice. Béla was tempted to try and cross over into the city because he had always wanted to see the canals, but he was almost completely broke and tired and dirty, so he found an empty garage in the industrial area of Mestre on the mainland where he slept that night and, the following morning, he hitched a ride with a farmer who had sold his produce in the early morning market along the Laguna Veneta and was heading back to his fields outside Udine.

Fortune smiled on Béla when that particular farmer stopped to give him a ride. The man, whose name was Giorgio in Italian, but also Georg in German, because he, like many in the far northeast of Italy, identified with being ethnically Austrian and spoke German as his first language. He had blond hair and blue eyes, a full mustache, long sideburns and he wore a stained, loden green *cappello* at a rakish angle, decorated with a soft 'brush' fashioned from the hair of a chamois goat.

Once Georg realized Béla spoke no Italian, he tried German and, since Béla was fluent in Yiddish and passably coherent in German, they were able to have a conversation.

Béla spun out a story that he was a Hungarian who had settled in Israel after the end of the war and was now travelling to Austria to reunite with his brother whom he had not seen in ten years and who fled Budapest during the brief Hungarian Revolution. Georg, wise to the subtleties of European mixed heritages and sympathetic to Béla's story, did not press for details and, more or less, accepted Béla's narration as true. He offered to let Béla stay at his farmhouse for the night and Béla gladly accepted.

After a much-needed bath and, after that, a hearty three-course meal of thick vegetable soup, pasta and roasted chicken served by Georg's plump, good natured, pretty wife, Elsa, Béla and Georg sat on Georg's front porch with a view of the Carnic Alps in the distance, drinking Georg's home-brewed, wild cherry schnapps. Georg asked Béla how he was planning to get over the mountains.

Sensing a sympathetic ear, Béla explained that he had a serious problem since he didn't have a visa for Austria and he was afraid of being turned back if he tried to pass through the normal border controls.

"You are correct," said Georg. "You will be turned back. We are in a very sensitive area where the borders of Yugoslavia, Italy and Austria meet. The southeastern Austrians and northern Yugoslavs see themselves as Slovenians, and we northern Italians and our neighboring Austrians see ourselves as Tyrolean. All of us view the borders as artificial and there are many who would be inclined to make serious trouble to bring down these borders."

Béla grew even more concerned. "I didn't know this," he mumbled. After a moment he added, "Is it impossible to pass through?"

Georg laughed. "Impossible, no. In the mountains, no border is impossible to cross. But it can be difficult, especially this time of year."

"How difficult?"

"There are many police patrols from all three countries. Also, it will be much colder up there. It might snow, and the trails are steep and slippery."

"But one could get through?"

Georg shrugged. "One could get through," then he winked, "with the right help."

Béla caught the mood. "And where might I find that help?"

Georg laughed conspiratorially. "I think you have already found it."

The next morning, Elsa cooked them a large breakfast and packed a rucksack with thick slices of *prosciutto di San Daniele* and Montasio cheese. She also packed a flask of strong Refosco merlot and two freshly baked baguettes.

Georg drove high into the foothills where he parked his truck along the side of the road and he and Béla began their hike into the mountains. It was a chilly morning that grew ever more frigid as they climbed higher. Béla was grateful for the heavy jacket and hat that Georg had given him. Around noon, they stopped, ate their sandwiches and drank the bracing red wine. Béla was breathing heavily, unused to the altitude and heavy climbing. Still, he felt calm, refreshed, until he heard voices approaching, coming down the mountain.

"It's the *carabinieri* (national police) from Coccau Valico," warned Georg. "Don't say anything. Let me do the talking."

When the heavily armed police approached, Georg greeted them enthusiastically in Italian. The lead policeman returned his greeting, glanced toward the silent Béla, and then he spoke to Béla.

Georg interrupted: "That's my stupid oaf of a little brother. He refused to learn Italian as a young boy and now he doesn't understand and no one understands him." He made the classic hand sign to indicate he found his 'brother' slightly crazy.

The officer huffed. "He must learn. We are all Italian now."

"*Sì, sì, certo*" Georg agreed. "Would you share our wine with us?"

The policeman was tempted, but he declined. As the carabinieri continued their march down the mountain, the officer shouted over his shoulder, "Make sure he learns Italian. It will keep him out of trouble."

By late afternoon, dark ominous clouds gathered overhead. The light breeze grew heavier. Soon the wind was blowing hard and a thick fog enveloped the mountain. Béla pulled up the collar of his jacket to cover his neck better and pulled on the hat to cover his ears, just as it started to snow.

"We've cleared the summit," shouted Georg. "I can just barely see Caccau at the bottom of the gorge. We're near the border."

Béla only nodded. He was cold, weak and disoriented.

"We should meet up with the Gailitz River over that ridge." Georg pointed a hundred meters up to their left. "Can you make it?"

Béla nodded, although he wasn't sure that he could.

As they reached the ridge and climbed atop a flat rock, Béla could see a fast-moving, whitewater stream that tumbled over large boulders and dislodged pines. "We're here," Georg yelled. There was a big smile on his face as he pumped his fist and thumped Béla on the back.

Unfortunately, Georg's thumping caused Béla to lose balance. He slipped off the rock and down the muddy hillside, gathering speed as he headed for the river. So this is how it ends, thought Béla as he heard a splash and felt his head bang against a granite rock as he passed into unconscious darkness.

When he awoke some hours later, he saw a smiling face hovering over him, and he heard the words, "*Willkommen in Österreich, Adalbert* (Welcome to Austria, Adalbert)."

Shit! thought Béla, I'm in deep trouble if they speak German in Heaven. Then he passed out again.

Chapter Twelve: The Imposter

Di gantse velt shteyt af der shpits tsung.
The entire world rests on the tip of the tongue.
—Bernstein, Jüdische Sprichwörter und Redensarten.

Béla's greatest worry, how he would manage to get through the perimeter and into the Eisenstadt camp, would turn out to be no problem at all. Back in Israel, haunted by terrifying images of the death camps at Auschwitz, Bergen-Belsen and Buchenwald, Béla had imagined barbed wire, stone walls, double fences and guard towers. The refugee camp at Eisenstadt had none of these barriers. In fact, there were no barriers at all. One was free to simply walk into or out of Eisenstadt at will.

However, getting through Austria to Eisenstadt proved to be more difficult than Béla had anticipated. The stormy weather that fell upon Béla and Georg in the mountains continued to bedevil Béla after he left Georg in Arnoldstein and made his way toward Klagenfurt, a larger town on the shores of the Wörthersee. Monstrous black clouds rolled across the surrounding hillsides, lightening streaked through the heavy air, thunder rumbled in the distance down the valley and then crashed nearby as the rain pelted down upon a shivering, soaked Béla who stood on the edge of the road near Villach trying to thumb a ride from the passing cars and trucks—their drivers barely able to see him through the downpour. Finally, a grumpy farmer pulled over and signaled to Béla that he could ride in the back of the farmer's truck under a makeshift tarp that provided only minimal protection from the wind and rain.

When the farmer arrived in Klagenfurt, he stopped his truck in the center of the city, near the Schillerpark, and told Béla he should get out there. Béla pulled the tarp away and started to leave the truck when he saw the enormous 16th-century dragon statue facing him in the rain and he stopped mid-step. Although Béla was not usually superstitious, that ferocious medieval stone dragon, the bad fall in the mountains, hunger, cold and the continuing storm combined to convince him that leaving the truck would be his downfall. He refused to move. The farmer yelled at Béla. Béla just stood there, immobile in the truck bed. The farmer wasn't about to get totally soaked himself so he shrugged his shoulders, returned to the cab and drove off, nearly tumbling Béla onto the street.

Their next stop was the farmer's home in the tiny village of Oberwuchel on the road toward Wolfsberg. The farmer parked his truck in the muddy grass near a tidy, tile-roofed house and this time he demanded Béla leave the vehicle. He guided Béla to a wooden barn, which was dry, and left him there next to a large brown-and-white cow with big ears, a dozen or so clucking, pecking chickens and a faded red tractor. A few minutes later, the farmer returned with blankets, a flask of beer, a loaf of black bread and a chunk of hard cheese. Then, he shut the barn doors and left. When Béla realized the farmer wasn't coming back, he stripped off his wet clothes, hung them out on wooden railing to dry, wrapped himself in the blankets and dropped off to sleep, too tired to eat the cheese or drink the beer.

Very early the next morning, the farmer arrived to milk his cow and gather eggs from his chickens. He used the toe of his boot to rouse the sleeping Béla and told Béla he would have to leave. Béla awakened, drank the beer, ate the cheese and bread, dressed in his still damp clothes and wandered over to the truck. Since it was still drizzling, the farmer allowed Béla to sit in the truck's cab while he drove Béla to the main road. Béla stumbled out of the truck and stood by the side of the road, a damp ghost in the early morning gray mist.

His next ride came from a truck driver delivering crates filled with screeching piglets to a slaughterhouse on the outskirts of Wolfsberg. After a few minutes, the driver began to ask questions and Béla repeated the story he had told Georg back in Italy, that he was a Hungarian refugee from WWII who was travelling to Austria to reunite with his brother whom he had not seen in ten years and who fled Budapest during the brief Hungarian Revolution For some reason he did not include the information that he was Jewish.

The driver pulled out a pack of cigarettes and offered one to Béla who declined. The driver was in a talkative mood and he continued to question Béla, as thick blue cigarette smoke enveloped him. Béla kept answering the questions and suddenly the truck driver said, "Your German is strange."

Béla said, "I am Hungarian. I have an accent."

The driver said, "I don't mean your accent. You use strange words that are not German. I think you are a Jew."

"*Ja*," said Béla, "*Ich bin ein Jude.*"

The driver slowly pulled his truck over to the edge of the highway. "*Aussteigen!*

(Get out)," he told Béla. "*Schweine liefere ich nur in Käfigen.* (I do not deliver pigs who are not in cages.)"

Béla, who had not experienced such virulent insults since he left Romania, was completely unprepared for the driver's sudden outburst. He felt like he had been slapped across the face. As he exited the truck, he spat on the floor. "*Es iz ir vas zenen der khazir* (It is you who are the pig)," he deliberately said in Yiddish, but the driver got the message.

His next ride was with a young woman driving a battered Volkswagon Beetle. "*Ich bin ein Jude,*" said Béla as he defiantly sat down in the passenger seat.

The startled woman shook her short curly brown hair, adjusted her steel-rimmed glasses and broke out laughing. "*Und wohin soll's gehen, wanderndes Jude* (And where might you be travelling, wandering Jew)?"

Béla relaxed under the sunshine of her smile and recited his story yet again. The young woman then told Béla that she was, in fact, also going to Eisenstadt to deliver food and clothing she'd collected to be given to the refugees. Béla looked over his shoulder and noticed the rear seat of the little Beetle was crammed with cardboard boxes and paper bags. Then Béla glanced over at the girl's freckled face. He smiled at her curly hair and odd round glasses. Cute, he thought to himself, but he also knew he was rumpled, filthy and old enough to be her father, so he said little.

As they approached the large city of Graz, Béla did ask her how difficult it would be to get into the camp at Eisenstadt. The girl, who told him her name was Ursula, shook her head briefly, confused by Béla's question. "There is no problem getting into the camp," she said, "It's a large old army base with wooden dormitories but no guards or fences." She seemed to consider some unknown thought for a moment. "You might, however, have some trouble finding your brother."

Béla said nothing.

"I could help you find him," said Ursula. "I have met the people who run the camp. I know my way around."

Béla said nothing.

Ursula noted his silence. "What's wrong?" she asked.

Béla knew he had to say something. "I'm just thinking about seeing my brother. It's been a long time."

"Oh," she said. "Yes, of course."

They drove through Graz without stopping. As they left the city behind, Ursula asked Béla if he was hungry. Béla said no, but the girl responded that even if he wasn't hungry, she was. As they drove out of the rolling hills and thick forests onto the flat farming plain approaching Wiener Neustadt, Ursula pulled into a gravel parking area that surrounded a small country café. The rain had stopped, the weather was relatively mild and so they sat down at an outside, rough, wooden table under a large elm tree.

Béla was uncharacteristically quiet and pensive as they ate ham and cheese sandwiches, washed down by strong apple cider. Ursula studied Béla with some curiosity, but she respected his silence. Béla finished eating and raised his eyes toward Ursula. "I have no money," he said sadly.

"Ach," she said dismissively, flashing her lovely smile, "so, that's the problem. Please, don't worry. I will pay."

"I'm sorry," said Béla. He hesitated. "I need to use the bathroom."

Ursula laughed. "Of course. I will still be here."

"I'm really very sorry," Béla said again. His overly emotional apology again pricked Ursula's curiosity.

Béla carried his knapsack with him as he walked around to the back of the restaurant. He relieved himself, washed his face and hands in the tiny sink, swung his pack over his shoulder and ran as fast as his tired old legs could carry him through a surrounding hay field, toward a stone fence and a stand of pine trees. He leapt over the fence and dropped to the ground. After he caught his breath, he took a chance and peeked over the stones toward the café. Ursula remained waiting patiently under the elm. Béla placed his knapsack under his head to rest for a minute, closed his eyes and fell into a deep sleep. When he awakened hours later, the clouds had returned and Ursula was gone.

Although the wind picked up and the sky grew even darker, it didn't rain, but Béla was, nonetheless, cold. He opened his knapsack and checked his crumpled, torn map. It appeared he was less than 50 kilometers from Eisenstadt, so he wandered back over to the main road and was able to catch a ride with a family who were driving toward a campsite near the Neusiedler See. They dropped him off outside the small village of Mattersburg. At that point, he was less than 15 minutes from Eisenstadt. But it was late and he didn't want to chance running into Ursula, so he curled up on a bed of pine needles under the moonless sky and fell into a restless sleep, hoping it wouldn't rain during the night.

At daybreak, he awakened to thick, damp fog, but no actual rain. Still, he was miserable, but he decided the best tactic was to hike into the refugee camp so that he would appear to truly be a straggling refugee who somehow made his way through the closed Hungarian border despite the patrols, the barbed wire and the guard towers. He certainly looked the part. He had grown a scraggly beard, his clothes were torn and dirty, he was very thin, hungry, thirsty, his eyes were droopy, his shoulders slack, defeated.

It was late afternoon when he finally reached the Eisenstadt camp. He stumbled into the muddy entrance area and collapsed beneath the wooden overhang that protected the main office from the unpredictable weather. An older man and a young woman who were shuffling papers in the office noticed this strange-looking man collapse near the door. They were immediately concerned because Béla actually arrived in far worse condition than the comparatively well-fed, decently dressed, relatively clean refugees who had fled Hungary months earlier. The woman ran outside and cradled Béla's head in her lap. Béla looked up into her kind eyes. "*Hol vagyok?* (Where am I?)" he muttered in Hungarian.

"*Ön biztonságban van* (You are safe)," the young woman replied, also in Hungarian, as Béla began to shake and cough and sneeze uncontrollably. "*De el kell menni a betegszobába, azonnal* (But you need to go to the infirmary, immediately)!"

Intentionally or not, Béla's strategy to arrive at the camp sick and worn down provided him with a chance to get oriented in the protected environment of the infirmary rather than being immediately exposed to the scrutiny of the camp officials or other refugees. He used that time wisely to study the routines within the camp and to listen to the stories of the patients in the infirmary. He offered little or no information about himself and allowed others to assume his rectitude came from being exhausted after his long ordeal, which was in fact true enough, although it was not the ordeal everyone else thought he had experienced.

Béla had also been speaking Hungarian often enough in Israel that he was comfortable with the language of his youth and so, when he left the infirmary after six days and moved into the general population, he found that no one considered his language skills suspicious. His first real problem came with the realization that almost all the Hungarians in the camp were from Budapest or its environs and Béla had never even been to Budapest, so he decided to adopt the persona of a peasant from eastern Hungary near Debrecen, where he had never been either, but neither, it seemed, had any of the other residents of the camp.

Once he found a bed in one of the long, narrow, wooden men's dormitories, Béla settled comfortably into the lazy, boring rhythms of refugee life. There was really nothing to do and nowhere to go, so inhabitants spent most of their time eating, sleeping, gossiping and trying to figure out what they were going to do next. Béla knew the routine. It was more or less like the immigration centers in Haifa.

A large contingent, in fact the majority, of those in Eisenstadt were content to integrate into Austrian society if they were given the opportunity, especially into

Vienna where there were already large numbers of citizens of Hungarian descent from the days of the old Austro-Hungarian Empire and life in Vienna was a relatively easy transition from life in Budapest. But Béla had no interest in becoming an Austrian citizen or living in Vienna. His dream was America, or Canada if necessary, so he was focused on trying to figure out how he could apply for asylum.

Sometimes, late at night when he couldn't sleep, he wandered around outside his dormitory, under the stars, and thought about his precious daughter Rita and his amazing Fanny, the two of them abandoned and alone back in Rehovot, and he was so overwhelmed with guilt and nostalgia that he had to sit down on a bench or he would faint from the emotional pain and disorientation. Once seated, he would stare into the crisp, clear nighttime sky and conjure up visions of the three of them settled comfortably into a sprawling brick American suburban house with a great green lawn and huge oak trees, like the houses he'd seen in magazines, and there were dogs for Rita and a shiny black car in the driveway for him to drive, and his enjoyment of his fantasy was so delicious that it would momentarily chase away the emptiness in his heart. But only momentarily, so Béla redoubled his efforts to apply for asylum.

Filling out the immigration forms was easy enough. Not having Hungarian documentation was a bit of a problem, but not an insurmountable one given what he had supposedly experienced in order to escape from eastern Hungary into Austria. But he was worried about the mandatory interview (there was always an interview) because he found that when he did talk to the others in the camp, he did not really fit in. For one thing, he knew too much. He revealed a knowledge of international affairs unusual for someone living in the closed environment of postwar Hungary and, especially so, for a peasant from Debrecen. Secondly, while he knew too much about the outside world, he appeared to know too little about the petty, day-to-day, bureaucratic inconveniences and secret humiliations of life under Hungarian Communism. He tried to pick up the nuances, but in the midst of a conversation, someone would stop talking and look at him strangely, as if they suspected something was amiss.

On the day he was scheduled for his interview, Béla stood in line with other refugees seeking asylum. No one talked much. They were all too nervous. When it was Béla's turn to enter the interview room, an older man, an American speaking excellent Hungarian, greeted him and requested that Béla take a seat in front of the plain, gray metal desk where the man was waiting for him. The man reviewed Béla's paperwork, then he said, "*Szóval, Mr. Izsák, akkor te vagy zsidó?* (So, Mr. Izsák, you are Jewish?)"

"*Igen* (Yes)," said Béla, somewhat startled.

"Lucky to be alive," said the American, continuing in Hungarian. "Not many from your part of Hungary survived."

Béla shrugged. He was very uncomfortable with this line of questioning.

"Of course, this is to your advantage, Mr. Izsák. I myself am Jewish from Transylvania. I escaped to England just before the Germans came and, from there, to America."

Béla nodded, wide-eyed. Inside, he was terrified.

The American continued. "As I said, I am very sympathetic to your situation, Mr. Izsák, whatever that situation truly is." He shuffled Béla's paperwork. Then, he set it aside. "So…what is your real situation, Mr. Izsák?"

Béla began to sweat. His eyes darted around the small room. His mind was racing, desperate to try and figure out how much the American knew and how he, Béla, the great talker, might possibly wiggle out of this situation.

The American smiled, "*A macska bekapta a nyelvedet?* (A cat got your tongue?)" Béla was rigid. Then the American spoke in Yiddish, "*Vos kenen nit ir entfern mir* (Why can't you answer me)?"

Béla knew he was doomed, but still he said nothing.

Unbeknownst to Béla, the camp was infiltrated with spies; Soviet spies trying to mingle with the refugees to exploit the opportunity to gain entry into the US, and American spies trying to discern who might actually be Soviet spies.

"Well," said the American, "we also know that you are not who you told us you are, because I have spoken with a young woman who volunteers to help us here in the camp. You told her you were looking for a brother who escaped from Hungary, so, obviously, you are not the one who escaped Hungary."

The American stood and walked over to another door to the right of his desk. When he opened it, Ursula entered and stood facing the seated Béla.

"I waited for over an hour," she said quietly.

Béla hung his head. The other two couldn't see the tears forming in his eyes.

"I tried to help you," said Ursula, "and that was how you repaid me?"

Béla's shoulders shuddered. He sniffled. He repeated over and over in three different languages, "I'm sorry, I'm sorry, I'm so sorry." Then he broke down completely. "I don't know why I lied. What difference does it make? I just want to go to America. Please! I want to live in America with my family."

The American rested a hand softly, sympathetically on Béla's shoulder. "Go back to Israel, Mr. Izsák. Go home to your wife and daughter. America doesn't need you. But I think maybe they need you."

Years later, whenever Béla would speak about this episode, he would laugh and say, "I almost made it, but I got caught because of my big mouth." Then he would add more wistfully, "My mother used to say that you need to strike the iron when it's hot. When I read in the newspapers about the Hungarian revolution, I immediately saw the once-in-a-lifetime opportunity for me to escape my hardships in Israel. I strwcked the iron, but I got burned…"

Chapter Thirteen: Chastened Return to Eretz Israel

Mit eyn por fis ken men nit tantsn af tsvey khasenes.
You can't dance at two weddings with one pair of feet.
— Stutchkoff, Der Oytser fun der Yidisher Shprakh.

The Americans didn't want Béla, so they handed him over to the Austrians. Béla didn't want the Austrians, so the Austrians promptly drove him to the border and turned him over to the Italians and, since his visa had expired, the Italians didn't want Béla either, so they put him on a ship to deliver him to the Israelis. That was how Béla found himself back on the rust bucket *Aliya*, chugging across the Mediterranean toward Haifa.

It would be an understatement to describe Béla as unhappy. He was despondent, exhausted and humiliated by the failure of his grand scheme. To make matters worse, he was travelling on a ship filled with American, French and Italian Jews brimming with joy and optimism about creating a new life in Israel and determination to build their young nation into a strong and vibrant country. Béla remembered when he had felt that way, and the loss of that optimistic fervor saddened him.

He was also very apprehensive about reuniting with Fanny and Rita. He had convinced himself that they would be overjoyed to join him in America in their spacious suburban home with the large lawn and a big black car in the driveway, but how would they feel about taking him back into their apartment in Rehovot after he had abandoned them without even telling them where he was going or why he was leaving. In his heart, he didn't truly believe he deserved to be welcomed back. He was terrified that Fanny might have already found a younger man who was an educated scientist from the Institute and a good prospective father figure for Rita. Dozens of nightmare scenarios filled his head as he wandered about on deck trying to relax and breathe in the fresh sea air.

Suddenly he felt himself jostled by two young bearded men speaking American English. The taller of the two stopped to apologize. "Sorry," he said and nodded toward Béla.

The shorter, stouter one held out a hand to Béla. "We're going to Israel. My name is Ezra," he added. "My friend's name is Nathan."

But Béla was still lost in his discouraging thoughts, and he ignored the man.

Ezra was perplexed by Béla's attitude and his apparent unwillingness to shake hands. He misinterpreted Béla's confusion as hostility. "What's the matter with you?"

"We said we're sorry we bumped you," said Nathan.

Béla still said nothing. He had no command of English at this point in his life. He was disoriented and overwhelmed with foreboding. Moreover, just as they misinterpreted Béla's behavior as hostility, he misinterpreted their brash, American style as aggression. When Nathan attempted to put an arm around Béla's shoulder in a friendly gesture, saying, "Come on, we're all going to the Holy Land together…," Béla aggressively pushed Nathan's arm away and accidently elbowed Ezra. The smaller man, startled and increasingly annoyed by Béla's actions, pushed Béla backwards, and added, "asshole!"

Béla had had enough. He regained his balance and charged toward Ezra, fists flying. Nathan moved quickly to grab Béla from behind and wrestle him to the ground. As Béla attempted to kick himself free, his ankle slammed against the deck railing and intense pain shot up his leg and registered on his brain. At that point, he had no more fight in him as he rolled over onto his back and groaned. His ankle was clearly broken as was his spirit.

To the Americans' credit, they tried to make amends by helping carry Béla to the infirmary and they explained to the ship's doctor what had happened. The doctor confirmed the obvious, a broken bone, and gave Béla a small packet of painkillers, set his ankle in a cast and provided Béla with an old set of wooden crutches that another passenger had left on board during a previous voyage. Unfortunately, the crutches were too small and Béla was forced to hunch over when he tried to stand upright, but they were better than nothing, so Béla took the crutches.

The next morning the *Aliya* arrived in Haifa and Béla hobbled down the gangplank onto land. Back in Israel. Exhausted. Broke. Crippled.

Béla knew he had to go to Rehovot, but he was in no hurry to get there. After he passed through customs, he wandered aimlessly around the port area, watching the cargo ships load and unload. He sat down on a pallet of canned goods containing, as best he could make out, peaches from Poland. Before long, another man, roughly his age, sat down next him. He had curly dark hair, a short beard and a sunburned face. He wore dark glasses, khaki shorts and an unbuttoned blue short-sleeve shirt. "Apricots," said the man.

Béla turned toward the stranger, "What?"

"Apricots," repeated the other man. "We're sitting on cans of apricots from Poland. Amazing."

"Oh," answered Béla in fractured Hebrew, "I thought they were peaches."

"No," said the man. "They're apricots. We should be eating Communist apricots? No! We should grow our own apricots. We should be sending our apricots to Poland."

Béla had nothing to add to that declaration. The two men sat in silence for a moment. Then the stranger pointed toward Béla's cast. "What's wrong with your leg?"

Béla didn't say anything.

"Were you working on the Hula Valley project? It's an amazing thing this project. Taking all that swamp land and turning it into farm land. It's a great achievement, something to be proud of. This is how Israel will be able to send apricots to Poland."

"Uh…"

"I am curious, was the work on the Hula stopped when the Sinai War started? I imagine many workers were drafted for the war."

Béla was in Israel when the Sinai War broke out in October 1956. The Israelis, the French and the British had invaded Egypt to capture the Suez Canal and topple the Egyptian President, Gamal Abdel Nasser. Béla followed these developments closely, but then the news about the Hungarian revolt captured his attention and landed him in his present sad state of pain and shame.

"We sure are getting fucked over by the Americans and the Russians, forcing us to withdraw when we were already only 16 kilometers away from the Suez Canal. Well, fuck them. Next time we'll sweep across the desert all the way to Cairo and destroy the fucking Arabs, right?" The man was laughing, but then he pointed again at Béla's foot. "Sorry you got hurt. Sorry about that."

Béla thought for a moment. If he was going to live in Israel again, he wanted to start out truthfully. "I wasn't on the job in the Hula Valley," he said. "I broke my ankle traveling on a boat from Naples."

"New to Israel, then?"

"No, returning."

Now it was the stranger's turn to be confused.

"I wanted to leave," said Béla. "I had to get out of this place."

The man was astonished. "Why would you want to leave paradise?"

"It's not paradise for me," said Béla, sadly.

The man angrily stood up and faced Béla. "If you weren't already hurt, I'd beat the crap out of you," the man spit at Béla's feet. "If you want to live here, you better change your attitude, *schmuk*." Then he stalked off, stopped, turned, flipped Béla the finger and then continued on his way.

Béla wanted to be angry as well, but he knew that, basically, the stranger was right. If he was going to live in Israel, he needed to change his attitude. If he was going to go back to his family, he needed to change his attitude. If he was going to be a good husband and father, he needed to change his attitude. He knew he needed to put all of his pain and anger and frustration behind him and be the man he was during his good times back in Bucharest.

As he sat there on the pallet of apricots, remonstrating with himself, he realized his ankle was throbbing intensely. He took two of the painkillers the ship's doctor had given him and within minutes he felt better. So it was with renewed hope and resolve that he stumbled over to the road and leaned on his old wooden crutches in order to hitch a ride to Rehovot.

Because he did look like a wounded veteran that, in fact, he wasn't, a truck driver immediately pulled over to the side of the road, hopped out of his cab and helped Béla climb into the passenger seat.

"Where are you going?" asked the truck driver.

"Rehovot."

"I can take you as far as Tel Aviv."

Once the driver re-entered the highway, Béla was immediately confronted with a situation where he had to make a decision about his promise to tell the truth when the driver asked him, "So, what happened to you? Were you wounded in the skirmishes?"

Béla pondered his choices, and then, in the best *shtetl* tradition, he reasoned he could still answer honestly by saying, "There was a fight," because the driver didn't ask where Béla was actually fighting.

"So tell me how you got wounded?"

Again, Béla was able to walk the thin line between fact and fiction by saying, "I don't want to talk about it," which was, of course, also true because he didn't.

Thankfully, the truck driver was willing to resist asking any more questions and the remainder of the trip was uneventful.

As the truck approached the northern outskirts of Tel Aviv, the driver told Béla he was going east toward *Rosh HaAyin*, so he would leave Béla on the main highway where he was likely to again get a quick ride south toward Rehovot. This time, despite his crutch and forlorn appearance, Béla did not get a ride that quickly and as he stood along the road in the broiling sun, his ankle began to throb and a sharp cramp developed in his calf muscles. He took two more pills, felt somewhat light-headed and thought he might just want to sit down in the dust for a while, when a small car pulled over. The driver, a slightly-built man with a neatly trimmed beard and wearing a yarmulke, was gentle and patient as he loaded Béla into his car.

"Where are you going?" asked the driver.

Béla told him he needed to get to Rehovot.

"What do you think?" asked the driver when they were settled in and on their way.

Béla, who was half delirious from the pills, had no idea what the man was talking about, so he just shook his head.

"Of the car…" said the man. "This is an Israeli-built car, made in Haifa. Wonderful, no? Soon we'll be shipping them to America."

Again Béla didn't have any opinion about that, so he said nothing.

"We Israelis can do anything," the man added, "although I do wish we could stop fighting and get along with the Arabs." He looked over at Béla. "You were in the war, weren't you?"

Béla knew he should say something, but he was so drowsy he simply nodded off to sleep.

"They're not all bad," the man continued, "the Arabs. Someday we will have to get along or…" But Béla was snoring.

When the driver attempted to awaken Béla as the car approached Rehovot, Béla was dreaming about his American suburban house, his new car and his happy family standing at the front door waving him home after a long day's work. Then, he was dimly aware of being shaken and someone's voice repeating over and over, "Rehovot."

Béla opened his eyes, but he still didn't know where he was. His head felt like it was floating separately from his body and his vision was hazy. Occasionally, swirling patterns danced from left to right and small dots would burst into tiny multi-colored eruptions. He tried to smile with delight at the light show, but his lips were numb, uncontrollable. He felt a small sliver of saliva drip from the left corner of his mouth, but his hand couldn't find his mouth to wipe the drip away. He vaguely heard the driver ask where he should let Béla out. Béla tried to focus on the landscape along the road, but he was distracted by the fascinating explosions that occurred each time he blinked his eyes.

The driver continued to prod Béla back into full consciousness and Béla finally realized where he was and what the driver wanted. Béla signaled that they should proceed further on along *Rehov HaRashi* (the Main Street). Then Béla waved his hand to indicate a left turn on *Rehov Yaakov* and then, after two kilometers or so, a right turn onto *Rehov Menuha VeNahala*, up a hill and then downhill, when Béla finally recognized Madam Traivish's estate.

The driver helped Béla out of the car and braced him as Béla stood tottering on his crutches, still heavily under the influence of consuming too many painkillers.

"Enjoy your ride? Great little car, no?"

Béla was still shaky on his feet and the little man wanted to walk Béla to his apartment, but Béla kept shaking his head, no. He didn't want a witness to his homecoming. So the driver reluctantly left Béla alone and drove off, while Béla began the short walk and long emotional journey toward his home that he was no longer certain was still his home.

As he approached the apartment, he first saw Rita running out of the house. He stopped, trembling with excitement to see her coming toward him. But then she veered off toward the neighbor's apartment and he vaguely understood she wasn't running to greet him. She didn't even see him. Then she stopped abruptly and stared at him. She was obviously startled by the gaunt, scruffy figure walking on crutches haltingly toward her, so she did an immediate about-face and sprinted back toward the apartment to get her mother.

When Rita re-appeared, holding onto her mother's hand, Béla made no move to retreat. He simply stood silently, an idiotic grin on his face as he swayed precariously, hunched over on his crutches, back and forth, left to right.

Slowly, Fanny's expression changed as a spark of recognition registered in her consciousness. "Oh my God!" she whispered to herself.

Fanny was simultaneously wracked with disbelief, anger, fear and tenderness as she moved toward the sad figure huddled in front of her. Béla, tears in his eyes, let go of his crutches and raised his arms to embrace her but, instead, he lost his balance and crumbled into the dirt at her feet.

Fanny was upset, a part of her wanted to kick the man crouched on the ground, but the strong woman inside her instead knelt down next to Béla, gathered him in her arms. "You have returned to us." She looked into his eyes. "You old fool."

Rita watched her mother with some uncertainty; then she said: "What happened to you, *Tata*?"

Béla couldn't answer her. He simply reached out his hand and wrapped his daughter's fingers in his palm. They sat together like that for a few moments; then Béla reached into his knapsack and held up two large red apples he'd brought from the boat to give to Rita. She smiled and immediately bit into one of the apples and the taste brought an even wider smile to her face. She laughed, "Wow, where did you find these? I've never seen such big apples before. And they are so sweet. Thank you, *Tata*."

Then Béla remembered the packet of postcards he'd bought in Rome that he intended to give to Rita when she and Fanny joined him in America. He brought out the postcards and, although they were a little worse for wear, Rita carefully studied each one and then took the packet and placed them in her treasure box that she kept under her bed. In the days to come, Rita often removed the cards from the box and marveled at the wonders her father had seen in a place called Italy. In the process, she created her personal memory that she could understand about where her father had been and why he left for so long.

Over the next two months, Béla quickly recovered physically. He had always been a strong man and he pushed himself with unwavering determination. He ate well, exercised constantly and helped Fanny with all the chores he had abandoned unattended. The family returned to taking their weekend trips to the beach at Bat-Yam, and Béla once again carried Rita on his shoulders as he swam to *HaSella* across the lagoon.

Things returned to normal, more or less. Rita was delighted to have her father back, but it was much more difficult for Béla to repair his relationship with Fanny. One evening, after Rita was in bed asleep, Fanny and Béla sat outside on their patio, drinking a glass of cold sweetened lemonade, enjoying the gentle breeze that rustled the leaves on the Eucalyptus trees. A big fat moon sat on the horizon just to the left of Madam Traivish's house. The evening star, Venus, shone brightly almost directly overhead, and the band playing in the reception hall behind the apartment, as if on cue, turned from raucous dance music to sentimental ballads.

"I'm sorry about…" Béla began, but Fanny raised her hand to cut him off.

"No more 'sorrys'," she said as she shook her head. "It's over. Done. Finished. I don't want you to talk about it. I don't want to hear anything about what happened."

"Alright," agreed Béla, "alright." He reached out his hand to cover hers. "But, Fannika, will you ever forgive me?" he asked.

"Probably not," said Fanny, matter-of-factly. "But I really am able to put this behind us. If for no other reason, then for Rita's sake."

Béla nodded. He was silent for a while. Then he asked, somewhat sheepishly, "Can we sleep together again?"

"We'll see how things go," said Fanny.

"How about tonight?" said Béla.

"Not tonight," said Fanny. Then she laughed when she saw Béla's reaction to her refusal. "But maybe tomorrow night," she said. She grinned flirtatiously. "Maybe tomorrow. We'll see."

Chapter Fourteen: A Furrier Again

Der seykhl iz a krikher.
Understanding grows at a snail's pace.
— Bernstein, Jüdische Sprichwörter und Redensarten.

It didn't take long for Béla to decide that if he was going to make a success of his second *aliya*—his second return to Israel—he was going to have to find work that he was proud to do and would make him happy. He wasn't going back to selling blocks of ice from a horse wagon. He certainly wasn't going to be tarring roofs again. And he was smart enough to know that he wasn't going to be doing something that required the educational credentials that Fanny had pursued.

Even before Béla left on his ill-fated journey, he had set up a large wood workbench in the yard behind the apartment, where he labored on occasional small jobs repairing or altering the furs that Rehovot's recent Jewish immigrants had brought with them from Europe. These alterations mostly involved shortening the long fur coats that served their owners well in the cold, long winters of Europe but were not practical for the mild winters in Israel. Occasionally, the well-off descendants from the early pioneers, the owners of orchard groves and olive groves and processing plants, would also place orders with Béla, for a kimono fur jacket or a collar coat or a shawl. Béla was excited to take on any job, small or large.

Rita used to watch Béla as he worked with the pelts. He enjoyed every step in the application of his old trade skills, progressing methodically and patiently through the various stages required to create the final product that he could be proud of.

He would start with spreading out on a workbench the assortment of fur pelts available for a particular job so he could examine the quality (thinness, coarseness) and appearance (wave pattern, sheen) of each individual pelt. He would select the nicest pelts to use in prominent areas of the garment and the lesser pelts for less visible areas and, in the process, he was already considering aspects of the final design.

The next phase involved using a furrier's special razor to cut each of the pelts lengthwise into narrow strips, one after another after another, and then resewing all the strips together, to reconstitute full pelts again. This seemingly absurd and tedious work, of first splicing and then resewing the splices back together, actually served a purpose. The order in which individual strips were rearranged and reattached, and the way they were reattached—sewing adjacent strips slightly staggered—helped the furrier achieve creative control over the ultimate appearance (wave and sheen) of the pelts. The sewing was done on a special fur sewing machine to produce fine, tight stitching.

In the next phase, Béla would also sew the reconstituted pelts, to create even larger sections, and then join these sections to create one large piece that later would be cut to the dimensions of a desired full-or-short-length coat or jacket or shawl. But before cutting this large piece according to a desired pattern, there was another phase to complete.

The large section of fur that resulted from the extensive resewing was too compact so the pelt required relaxing the skin by stretching. In order to loosen the seams of the too-tight sewing and to stretch out and enlarge even further this large section of fur, Béla would spread the section on the workbench, with the fur side facing down, the skin side facing up. Then, with a lightly moist sponge, he would first dampen the entire skin side, and proceed to pull hard on the edges of the skin, and to stretch it out in every direction. Then using a special furrier's stapler, he affixed the section onto the wood bench and let it rest in this way for several days. This part of the production was the most physically demanding. It would take several hours, standing hunched over the bench, exerting all the strength that Béla had, pulling on the tight fur section with one hand and using the other hand to staple the section to the workbench.

He had to repeat these actions at small intervals until the entire large section was fully stretched and fully tacked to the workbench. Later, after the staples were removed, the relaxed fur section, for the first time, would be cut to the desired dimensions and pattern of an order and fitted with a silk lining and trimmings (pockets and closing hooks). Lastly, to bring the fur back to life in the aftermath of such extensive handling and processing, Béla would use a hot iron and a furrier's iron comb to stroke the furry side, over and over again, until the hair was shining and flowing in just the direction that he willed it to go. It was then that the product was finally available to be fitted on the silhouette of a client.

Through these small occasional jobs, Béla's skill and artfulness, his Old

World know-how, won him admirers and more clients. Fanny couldn't help but notice that her husband was so obviously happy and involved when he was working with fur. Béla even took time to explain to Rita what he was doing and he set up simple tasks that his daughter could handle in order to help him. Whatever else he might be, Béla was a furrier.

The problem was that there wasn't at that point in time a commercial furrier business in Rehovot, nor was there much chance that being the first to open such a business would lead to success. There simply wasn't enough demand. That was why Béla had not seriously pursued his craft when the family first settled in Rehovot. But by early 1958, already ten years since the new state of Israel was formed, new economic opportunities loomed, and he reasoned, as he looked to find work, that Tel Aviv was only thirty-three kilometers away, an hour's commute at most by bus, and he thought there were enough rich, sophisticated urban Jews in Tel Aviv to support three or four furriers. Béla decided he would go to the big city and convince one of the shops to hire him. Something he now felt he should have done years earlier, but, as it is said, better late than never.

Béla started to take occasional bus rides to Tel Aviv even before his ankle was completely healed. Each time he made a trip to the city, Béla realized how much he missed the hustle and bustle of a large city. He might be a rural bumpkin deep down, but ever since he first wandered the streets of Bucharest as a young man, he was excited by the sounds of rumbling trucks and whirling motorcycles and honking taxis. He loved to smell the variety of scents from the Arabic, Israeli, Armenian and Greek restaurants—grilled meat, steamed vegetables, and boiled rice or couscous. He appreciated the smartly-dressed women and the alert, aggressive men. Everyone appeared to have somewhere to go and something to do. Being in Tel Aviv brought a smile to his face even as he limped from street to street looking for a place to work.

On his third trip to Tel Aviv, Béla was wandering down Allenby Street, the upscale, tree-lined commercial boulevard named after the British Field Marshal Edmund Henry Hynman Allenby, 1st Viscount Allenby, who, near the end of the First World War, defeated the Turks in numerous battles and helped end the hegemony of the Ottoman Empire over the Middle East. Béla began his job search where Allenby Street meets the Mediterranean Sea and he was walking toward the city center when he first saw a sign for Brown Furs. He entered the shop and he immediately knew that this was the place where he was going to work. But first, he had to sell himself.

Béla knew the routine: talk to the manager, explain his expertise with furs, especially his skills at splicing and reattaching the stripes to form creative designs, and his strong work motivation and then offer his services. But that wasn't so easy with a Tel Aviv furrier in the late 1950s.

At first, Béla was optimistic. The manager, a stocky, middle-aged man named Motl', born in the Galicia region of Northern Romania, seemed a good pairing with Béla. Although they greeted each other in Hebrew, they both quickly switched to Romanian when they recognized their common heritage. But just as Béla launched into his spiel about his expertise with furs, Motl' held up a hand to stop him.

"If you're here to find work, my friend, don't even try."

"But…," stammered Béla.

"You're looking for a pin in a hay wagon," said Motl'. "Not a week goes by when some immigrant, out-of-work furrier from the Old Country stops by to tell me I have to hire him because he's a master furrier with a magic touch."

"But…," insisted Béla.

"Béla, my friend, you seem like a nice guy, but Tel Aviv has 100 ex-furriers for every one fur buyer. We're living in the desert. Only the rich wear furs, and only to show off on formal occasions. And there aren't that many rich Jews in Tel Aviv," he said, and then he added, "or that many formal occasions either."

Béla was downcast, but not defeated. He knew he was going to work for Motl' at Brown Furs.

When Béla returned to Rehovot, he asked Fanny if her friend with the silver fox coat, the scientist from Odessa, still worked with her at the Weizmann.

"Nina? Yes, of course," said Fanny. "Why?"

"I repaired her fox coat last year."

"Yes, yes. She still talks about what a beautiful job you did."

"I need to borrow the coat. Will you ask her?"

So Fanny asked and Béla received. He took the coat with him on his next trip into Tel Aviv and brought the coat to Brown Furs where he displayed his repair for Motl' to see.

"This really is beautiful workmanship," said Motl'.

Béla beamed. "So, you have a job for me?"

"No," said Motl', "but the coat is beautiful. Would that my wife should have such a beautiful coat." After further thought, Motl' reconsidered: "Béla, you won't make much money here. It won't be like it was in Romania."

"It will be what it is," said Béla.

And so Béla began his career at Brown Furs and his daily commutes to Tel Aviv. Nina got her coat back and three months later Motl' received a wrapped package containing a beautiful fox fur collar that Béla made at his home workbench in Rehovot, for Motl' to give to his wife.

Béla prepared this collar from leftover scraps, same as he used to do when he was a young apprentice for Tálosi Mihály and he was caught and was accused of stealing from him. Over the many years that Béla worked at Brown Furs, he never saw the collar he made worn by Motl's wife and he was often curious on whose shoulders the collar actually rested.

While it was true that, in the beginning anyway, Béla did not make much money at Brown Furs, he was working again at work that he loved. In the evenings and on Saturdays he worked at home, making smaller specialty items—hats, collars, cuffs, trims—that became small treasures for the Rehovot women fortunate enough to be able to buy one. This became a lucrative side business that eventually brought in even more income for the family's savings. Béla was more relaxed. Rita enjoyed spending time with him as his "assistant" at the outdoor workbench and Fanny welcomed this new improved version of Béla into her bed at night.

As the years passed, the family's fortunes continued to improve. By 1962 (the same year that the infamous Nazi Adolf Eichmann, the SS officer who organized Adolf Hitler's 'final solution of the Jewish question' was hanged in Israel for his crimes against humanity, his body cremated and his ashes thrown unceremoniously into the Mediterranean Sea), the Izsáks had accumulated sufficient savings to enable them to leave behind their rented apartment in the poorer section of town, on the property owned by the nasty Madam Traivish who never really stopped torturing Béla during the entire time they stayed there.

With the purchase of the new apartment in the upscale part of town, adjacent to the entrance of the oasis that is the Weizmann Institute of Science, the Izsáks created a vastly improved living situation. The two-story building, with four generously proportioned units, was new, modern, comfortable—so different from the cramped quarters in the converted former stables, even with the improvised annex facility. Importantly, in those days before air conditioning, their new corner apartment had windows on four sides, which allowed good ventilation and cool breezes to pass through. A small orange grove extending along the side of the building saturated the apartment with the sweet scent of orange blossoms.

One big balcony faced a small garden and, beyond it, the short, quiet *Rehov Mohliver* (a street named after Samuel Mohilever, a 19th-century rabbi who encouraged Russian Jews to move to Palestine and develop settlements there). This small street connected *Rehov HaNasih* (named for Israel's first President) with the Institute. A second balcony, in the back of the apartment, faced a much larger garden, where in the spring, as the flowers came into bloom, two big trees transformed into thick green canopies. In the basement was an air-raid shelter.

The Izsáks finally attained the comfort that they longed for in Israel.

Fanny was extremely happy in her new home and very pleased with the position she secured at the Institute and the research work she did there. She had left behind her menial jobs packing oranges in the orchards and folding tablecloths in the factory. When she completed her education and training, she was hired by a rising young scientist, Professor M. Avron, who had studied in the United States and then received an appointment at the Weizmann. Fanny became his research assistant and collaborator in his newly established laboratory in the Biochemistry Department. It was her menial work that had sustained the family while Béla wandered recklessly around Europe, and it was mostly her new job and the mortgage loan guarantee from the Institute that provided the cash savings to buy the apartment.

It was Professor Avron who would invite her to go with him on several sabbaticals to the US, which would open new horizons, but also create new dilemmas, for the Izsáks. In fact, both Fanny and Prof. Avron benefitted from the official Israeli policy of supporting and promoting education and technology in the new nation. The former head of the Institute, Chaim Weizmann, also the first President of Israel and the man after whom the Weizmann Institute was named, had been a leading figure in advancing the concept that Israel's future would be determined by its people's brainpower, more than the nation's ability to turn the desert into a fertile garden, as the first wave of immigration had done. Weizmann firmly believed that whereas Israeli's past had been built on the agricultural *kibbutz* (cooperative), its future would rest on its science and technology.

Another component of the Israeli government's strategy was to encourage Israeli scientists and technicians to work and study abroad, both to increase individual knowledge and expertise, but also to spread throughout the world an awareness that Israel was intent on becoming a significant player in the scientific and technological revolution that was rapidly advancing the economic and commercial power of Europe and the United States.

In 1964, Fanny was offered an opportunity to accompany Professor Avron for a one-year sabbatical in the US, to work in the laboratory of the eminent Professor of Biophysics and Physical Biochemistry, Britton Chance, who was also the Director of the Johnson Foundation in the School of Medicine at the Ivy League University of Pennsylvania in Philadelphia. There was no question in Fanny's mind that she should accept the invitation, but acceptance meant temporarily moving the family to the United States. Ironically, she was set to accomplish Béla's dream at the very time when doing so meant she would disrupt his new-found happiness in Israel. She spent a few sleepless nights, mulling over that dilemma in her mind before she finally decided to talk to Béla and get his reaction.

At first, Béla was dumbfounded, a little bit intimidated and slightly annoyed. After all, he was supposed to be the one to bring his family to America. Since his failed effort in 1957 to reach the US and the period of deep frustration that followed, Béla regained his footing when he found a job with Brown Furs, working in the occupation that provided him with genuine satisfaction and ultimate sense of pride and self-esteem. To risk leaving might seem like tempting fate, like laughing in the face of good fortune. On the other hand, this could be his only chance to get to America and settle there once and for all.

"We're not moving there permanently," said Fanny, "It's only for one year."

"What if we want to stay there longer?"

"I don't want to live in America, Béla. I am happy in Israel. I love our new home. I am very happy working at the Weizmann Institute."

"And I am happy at Brown Furs, but I may not have a job if I leave for one year."

"Well, you could stay here if you want, but I am sure Rita will want to come with me even though she probably would like to graduate in the same year as her friends. And of course, there is that boy."

Béla was taken aback. "What boy?"

"Arie Schinnar. That good-looking boy who was actually born in the Bergen-Belsen Displaced Persons camp. The young man who's always skipping school and siting around in cafes, drawing political cartoons. Don't you pay attention to her at all?"

"I'm working all the time, Fanny."

"As am I, Béla." She stood before him, defiantly. "And I'm going to Philadelphia. What are you going to do?"

Béla wasn't sure how to answer. He was genuinely torn between the pull to go to America and the sensible decision to hang on to a job that he felt he was lucky to find after the earlier years of struggle. After a long silence, Béla cracked a smile. "You are asking me what I'm going to do, after all that I went through to get to America and I failed? You are asking me what I'm going to do now when I can go there legally? As I always say, 'hit the iron while it's hot.' I am going to America." He thought about his situation at Brown Furs. "I'll see what I can work out with Motl'. I once did him a big favor."

Béla did talk to Motl' and somewhere in their conversation there was mention of whatever happened to a certain fox fur collar, and Motl' assured Béla that there would be a job waiting for him when he returned from America.

Fanny almost changed her mind when she realized that leaving meant she would have to rent out their brand new apartment, a place that she had not even finished decorating to her taste. And she would have to rent it out to strangers. She didn't want strangers living in her home and so she was finding fault with every couple that came to apply. And there were lots of them. Housing in Israel was still in short supply, and this apartment was in a prime location and very appealing. Finally Béla said to her: "Fanny, are we going to America or not?"

"Of course we are."

"Then you have to rent our home, Fanny."

She walked away from him because she hated it when he told her what to do even if she knew she had to do it. And she did. She rented their home to an elderly woman from South Africa, the widowed mother of a scientist who had relocated his family to Israel and worked at the Institute.

So, in the summer of 1964—during the same year that Yitzhak Rabin was made Chief of Staff of the Israeli Defense Forces, and the PLO (the Palestinian Liberation Organization) was founded on the West Bank—the Izsáks took a taxi to Lod Airport (that would years later be renamed in honor of David Ben-Gurion, considered the primary founder of the modern state of Israel). There they boarded one of the newer El Al Boeing 707s and landed roughly ten hours later at John F. Kennedy Airport, newly renamed in honor of the assassinated American president. On their ride into the city, they caught their first glimpse of the awe-inspiring New York City skyline. Béla felt the hair rise on the back of his neck in child-like wonder that he was actually seeing the Empire State Building and the Chrysler Building and the recently completed Pan-Am Building. It was those hundreds of Hollywood movies that the Izsáks saw over many years that provided them with the easy familiarity to be able to identify the distinctive landmarks of New York City.

From the airport, the Izsáks arrived at the glorious old Penn Station—considered a masterpiece of the Beaux-Arts style and one of the architectural jewels of New York City—just as it was being demolished in what is still considered a great architectural travesty. Béla was overwhelmed by the chaos of the massive destruction as well as the new construction, but Fanny efficiently purchased tickets and directed the family to the departure gate for the train to Philadelphia.

Two hours later, the Izsáks arrived at the massive 30th Street Station in their new home—Philadelphia, the City of Brotherly Love, home to the Liberty Bell and to Independence Hall, where the American Declaration of Independence and the Constitution were signed. Béla had finally, truly been transported to the heart and soul of America, only to realize, somewhat uncomfortably, that he could not understand a single word spoken by the crowds of people scurrying past him.

Chapter Fifteen: A Taste of the American Dream

Nor in kholem zaynen mern vi bern.
Only in dreams are carrots as big as bears.
— Kogos, 1001 Yiddish Proverbs.

The Izsáks arrived in Philadelphia during one of the most troubled summers in the city's history. After Martin Luther King's 'I Have A Dream Speech,' delivered during the historic civil rights March on Washington in August of 1963 and after the assassination of President John F. Kennedy in November of 1963, the United States was entering a decade of extreme racial tension and increasing civil disturbances that would spread across the nation and result in serious outbreaks of looting, burning and urban unrest in almost every major US city including, most notably, New York, Chicago, Boston, Detroit and Los Angeles, among others. A major outbreak occurred in Philadelphia at the end of August in 1964, just as the Izsáks were getting settled into their new life.

A woman named Odessa Bradford had stopped her car in the middle of an intersection in predominately African-American North Philadelphia and, for whatever reason, she refused to move the car or leave it. Then the police attempted to forcibly remove Ms. Bradford from her vehicle. At that point, a fight broke out between the citizens and the police while untrue rumors spread that a pregnant woman had been beaten by police officers. Fighting erupted all over North Philadelphia and by the time that the unrest ended three days later, 341 people were injured, 774 people were arrested and 225 stores were damaged or destroyed. That was not what Béla, Fanny and Rita had imagined could happen in America; not the America they knew from the movies.

It was also not the America that Béla and his family immediately experienced. When Béla, Fanny, and Rita walked on foot across town on their many expeditions to explore their new surroundings, they were oblivious to the unrest taking place, although they did find it puzzling that the streets were almost entirely empty. Those people who were out stared at the curious family who seemed completely unaware of the potential risk to themselves, but no one bothered to stop and warn them of the danger.

Their first adventure began when the family arrived late at night and they checked into a Sheraton Hotel near the campus of the university. The next morning, Fanny, who was always level-headed and reliable, announced that she couldn't get out of bed. She was excited before, but now her stomach was in knots and she was in a near panic about working in the laboratory of the University's famous Professor Chance. She would not get out of bed, and she would not leave the hotel room.

Leaving the anxiety-stricken Fanny in bed, Béla—an adult who knew no English at all—and Rita—a teenager who knew the rudimentary English taught in school, ventured out on their own to initiate the search for a place to rent.

It was a very hot and humid day, the likes of which they had never experienced in Israel. While Israel was hot, sometimes, very hot, it was seldom humid. Even so, Béla was, as usual, excited about his new adventure, and Rita was in an upbeat mood as she walked alongside him, in her first pair of low-heel shoes and a colorful mini-dress that attracted appreciative whistles from construction workers and breezy greetings from passersby.

The university housing office provided them with listings to check and Béla and Rita dutifully marched from one address to another, becoming increasingly distressed by the condition of the places they saw. They began to get the impression that Israel appeared better off than America. The houses they saw were formerly owned by affluent Philadelphians who had left the city for the suburbs. These once large houses were now converted into multi-tenant rentals for the students and visitors and they looked cramped and untidy. It was at the end of a frustrating long day when the clammy and exhausted Béla and Rita signed the lease for a plainly furnished, one-bedroom apartment without air conditioning, the sole virtue of which was its location three blocks away from the renowned Robert Wood Johnson Pavilion where Fanny would work, once she finally managed to pull herself together and get out of bed.

The next task was to find a school for Rita. The neighborhood where their apartment was located meant she was slated to attend West Philadelphia High School—a school with a poor reputation for both academics and safety, even without the racial tensions that were to flare out later that summer. After passing tests arranged for her by the school district, she was placed in an elite, public, magnet school—the Philadelphia High School for Girls—where they tailored a special curriculum for her, taking into account her advanced standing in subject matters such as algebra, science and French, but lower standing in subjects such as American history, Civics and English.

By the middle of August, Rita and Fanny were taken care of. However, no special provisions had been arranged for Béla who spoke no English and had no American job experience. Yet it was to be Béla who, arguably, ended up with the best deal of the three of them.

Since her high school classes would not begin until September, it was left to Rita to help Béla find employment. Béla himself had quickly realized that his fantasy of living his American dream was going to prove more difficult than he had imagined. Looking for a place to live in the city had convinced him that suburban homes with large green yards and chauffeur-driven big cars were not going to happen overnight, if they were to ever happen at all. But Béla came to this understanding with his usual optimistic good nature and he decided that he would find a job anyway and enjoy the hard work, whether it made him rich or not. He certainly didn't want to sit around the hot, uncomfortable apartment all day, doing nothing while Fanny was working and Rita was in school.

He and Rita began their search for the right furrier business in the fashionable central downtown shopping areas on Chestnut and Walnut Streets, also near the University of Pennsylvania and fairly convenient near to their apartment. They found beautiful shops with luxurious furs, but also managers and salespeople who could hardly be bothered to even provide them the time of day. Admittedly, they appeared an odd couple—a pretty, petite, dark-haired girl, attractively but not particularly fashionably dressed, speaking for her much older father who obviously spoke no English at all. Why would anyone want to hire the old man? Although Rita argued that her father possessed unique, Old World skills, no one was impressed and no one seemed to care.

They next tried the shops out near Bryn Mawr College along Lancaster Avenue (Route 30)—the Main Line—that served the exclusive, privileged 'old money' families of the upper class suburbs west of the city. As they rode the Paoli/Thorndale train line west, Béla finally saw the American affluence he had seen in magazines: endless canopies of leafy trees, large brick and stone houses, gated estates and massive greener-than-green lawns. Béla had never seen this sort of concentrated, large-scale wealth before, not in Hungary or Romania, not Italy nor Austria nor Israel. This was the America he had dreamed about and he was amazed, even delighted, like a small child in a candy store who had always imagined, but never quite conceived his dream in all its glory. But Béla's delight provided no benefits. There was no work along the Main Line either: the timing was bad, it wasn't high season; the store had all the work staff that it needed; the language barrier was a serious obstacle.

They next took the Landsdale/Doylestown train north to Jenkintown, another well-to-do suburban area, but one somewhat more mixed socially and economically than the Main Line. Still, both Béla and Rita were acquiring an education about how much money existed in the Philadelphia area and to what degree this wealth contrasted with the conditions in the poorer urban areas closer to where they lived in the city. They were also starting to feel their initial optimism battered by the constant negative reaction to their attempts to find work for Béla.

Near the end of the day, when both father and daughter were weary and anxious, they walked through the doors of a modest-looking, brick-and stone-faced shop. As they entered the apparently empty shop, their appearance triggered a soft bell tone that alerted a short, bald man to emerge from the back of the shop. He had the sleeves of his blue shirt rolled up to his elbows and a yellow tape measure draped around his neck. He had the habit of rubbing his hands in complicated circles as he spoke in a faint foreign accent.

"What can I do for you, folks?" he said cheerfully until he actually saw Rita and Béla and his instincts told him he wasn't going to make a sale with these two.

"My father is looking for work," Rita began, "and he has…"

"I know, I know," the man interrupted, "Old World skills."

Rita was annoyed. "Well, he does. He's very skilled."

"Hey, I'm sure he is, young lady, but can't he talk for himself?"

"He doesn't speak English."

The bald man waved his hands in the air in exasperation. As he did so, Rita noticed faded numbers tattooed on his left forearm. She gasped. "You were in Auschwitz!" she blurted out.

"Yes," he said.

"My grandmother—my father's mother was murdered in Auschwitz."

"May God avenge her blood…." the man murmured. Béla brightened when he heard the Yiddish expression, but the man continued. "I am sorry, but I have no work for someone who can't speak English."

"His hands are his words," pleaded Rita, "and he really wants to work"

"And I need to make a living," the man argued. "Hey, what can I do…what can I do. Things are not so terrific here either. I need someone who can sell as well as create."

Rita was crestfallen. She turned to leave, when the man said, "Look, I know some people in South Jersey. They're just starting up a new business." He took a pen and wrote the name and address on the back of his shop's business card. "Go see them. They need someone like your father."

"South Jersey?" asked Rita.

"In New Jersey. A state. Just across the river from Philly. Not so far."

So the next day, Rita and Béla took the Lindenwold train line, left the train in Haddonfield, New Jersey, and walked down the quaint tree-lined streets of a beautiful, well-preserved village first founded in the early 1700s. The village's Indian King Tavern, built in 1750 and now a New Jersey State Historical Site, was where the colonists declared New Jersey a free state and loyal to the Declaration of Independence in Revolutionary War America. Béla and Rita saw a charming hamlet, with a colonial-era downtown, obviously as rich as any they saw on the Main Line or Jenkintown. They began to believe all of suburban America looked like these upscale Philadelphia suburbs.

Béla, who often proclaimed that he didn't believe in God, had serious second thoughts when he and Rita finally met the Jewish couple that ran Wenger Furs in Haddonfield. The timing was perfect. The Wengers had opened an elegant new store just two months earlier, but it was not yet stocked or staffed. Rita no sooner explained why she and Béla were there and that Béla was a highly skilled furrier from Israel, classically apprenticed in the European tradition, when the Wengers threw open their arms, hugged and kissed both Rita and Béla, and on the spot hired Béla, despite the fact that neither of them spoke Yiddish or Hebrew, let alone Romanian, Hungarian or German. For some unknown reason, they were confident everything would work out.

"You must return tomorrow!" exclaimed Gloria Wenger, an attractive woman in her mid-forties with a sincere, open face and a ready smile.

"Yes, yes, you will start immediately," said Harold Wenger, a tall, good-looking man with an equally affable demeanor. "You're our new manager."

When Rita explained all of this good news to Béla, he was extremely energized, enthusiastic that things could happen so quickly and easily in America. Imagine, already, a manager. He decided right then and there that, just as he had always believed, this was the sort of country where he wanted to live. When Rita and Béla returned to Philadelphia, they were in a very upbeat mood, impatient to share their wonderful news with Fanny.

A few days later, Rita began school at the Philadelphia High School for Girls and that choice required her to commute by bus through some of Philadelphia's toughest neighborhoods along north Broad Street. The first few trips were very scary, noisy and upsetting experiences for Rita who previously, back in Israel, had only a short, pleasant walk to get to school. After a while, Rita became accustomed to her morning journey and even enjoyed sitting by the window and observing the street life she saw taking place in nearby neighborhoods: knots of men gathered in front of a corner grocery stores, drinking beer from cans covered by brown paper bags; old, stooped women entering and leaving storefront churches; dangerous but strangely attractive young men skipping school, smoking cigarettes and shooting basketballs on park playgrounds; toddlers laughing and playing as they walked to kindergarten with their adoring mothers.

Coincidentally, at the same time the Izsáks were getting settled into their year in America, a number of their relatives were finally allowed to leave Romania and emigrate to Israel. Béla's two older brothers, Lali and Feri, and his two younger brothers, Sanyi and Károly, along with their wives and children, arrived in Israel. Also, Fanny's father, the feeble Avraham who had somehow managed to survive despite being incapacitated from his stroke, and her younger two siblings—her brother Nelu and her sister Suca—had also been allowed to emigrate along with their spouses and children. However, Fanny's apparently healthier parent, her mother, Malvina, had died just shortly after Fanny left Romania with Béla, for Israel. A persistent sadness tagged at Fanny's heart that the mother that she loved was left behind, buried in a neglected cemetery back in Fălticeni.

The timing of this new exodus of Jews from Romania was unfortunate for Béla and Fanny because they were not able to be in Israel to welcome their families; but the timing was very fortunate for the families because they were among the last to leave under a program whereby Israel had been "purchasing" visas, at the rate of $3,000 per person, paid to the Romanian government, for Romanian Jews to be allowed to leave Romania and go to Israel.

However distasteful it might have been for Israel to 'buy' human beings, Israel was eager to welcome the 350,000 Romanian Jews (by far the largest surviving Jewish population outside Russia despite the hundreds of thousands who had been killed or shipped to Germany to die in the camps). Those survivors were trapped under the *Gheorghiu-Dej* Communist regime and unable to leave as a new wave of anti-Semitism threatened them, just as Fanny's brother, Așu, had foreseen it would. And the shaky Romanian government was more than happy to have the cash (or the equivalent in agricultural products and oil drilling equipment) while simultaneously ridding the country of a population they didn't really want and that really didn't want to be there.

A year later, in 1965, Nicolae Ceausescu would come to power in Romania, and he would stop the policy of allowing Jews to leave, so Fanny's and Béla's family members made it out just in time. By 1969, however, Ceausescu also resumed the trade in Jewish lives, so that by the time Ceausescu was overthrown and killed by firing squad in Tîrgoviște, Romania, on Christmas Day in 1989, there were very few Jews still resident in Romania.

Meanwhile, Béla prized his life in the United States and threw himself into his work at Wenger Furs. He and the Wengers frequently worked long hours as their business expanded quickly, and Béla's weekends were often spent in Haddonfield. Harold and Gloria Wenger trusted Béla's advice and suggestions completely. They relied on him and they were grateful for him, because Béla was, in many ways, the one individual most responsible for launching their very successful new business.

And Béla was in his element at Wenger Furs. He thrived on the Wengers' warmth and respect and, when he gained some proficiency in English, on his encounters with clients, situations where his own charm and enthusiasm worked their magic. Eventually, the Wengers begged Béla to remain with them beyond one year. They offered to provide the papers needed to apply for permanent residency. They tried to talk Fanny into accepting a permanent life in America. They tried to influence Rita to influence her parents. For his part, Béla's hopes for a positive experience in America were more than fulfilled. He wanted to stay, but Fanny wouldn't relent. She was determined to return to Israel.

The World's Fair in New York City in 1964/66—in many ways, the last great burst of uninhibited American optimism before the political upheavals and societal changes that were to engulf the country during the remaining years of the 20th century and on into the 21st—was drawing large crowds, and the Izsáks were among them. American companies dominated the fair that was a showcase of mid-20th-century American culture and technology. Many of the pavilions were built in a futurist architectural style heavily influenced by automobile culture, by the shape of jet aircraft, by the Space Age, and an optimistic view of the Atomic Age. Some of the pavilions were clearly shaped like the products they were promoting: such as the US Royal tire-shaped Ferris Wheel. Other pavilions were more abstract representations, such as the spheroid-shaped IBM pavilion designed by the architect Eero Saarinen, or the General Electric circular dome-shaped "Carousel of Progress," designed by Disney.

The Izsáks wandered around the fairgrounds wide-eyed and slack-jawed by the gadgets on display: computer terminals, video phones, animatronic life-like robots, space capsules and 70mm-wide screen films. As they approached the 12-story high, stainless-steel model of the earth, called the Unisphere, that still stands today near the Tennis Center in Flushing Meadows, Queens, Béla could not help but exclaim, "Fanny, I love this country." "It's such a long way from where I started my life in Gâlgău...," he mused. "I want to stay here forever."

At first, Fanny said nothing. Then Béla noticed the theme of the fair displayed beneath the Unisphere. "Peace Through Understanding. Yes," said Béla, "this is the new world. Safe from all the wars and fighting in the old world. A miracle. This is the best place."

Fanny had had enough. "We're not staying in America," she said. "Our life is in the other new land, Israel. Our families have moved there. My brothers and sister are there. Your brothers are there. I have a job I love. We just bought a beautiful new apartment. You want me to leave all that? No, I won't do it."

Fanny also reminded Béla, as she had done many, many times before, both when they were living in Israel and during their visit to the United States, that Israel was a special place. "Israel is the only place where Jews can live without fearing persecution. It is in the only place where Jews can live with dignity and pride."

Béla produced his most charming, persuasive smile, and raised his arms to encompass all the wonders displayed around them. "But Fanny, look…"

Fanny was not about to change her mind. "No," she said. "We're going home after a year. I don't want to talk anymore about it." And they didn't. Instead, they enjoyed the rest of the fair.

In the following months, they relaxed and spent more time together, taking trips to tour Washington DC, to the beach at Atlantic City, to Longwood Gardens in Pennsylvania, to museums, art festivals and concerts, and, in the process, all three members of the family grew much closer. Perhaps that was the real miracle of their stay in America. They began referring to themselves as 'The Three Musketeers'—the Hungarian/Romanian/Israeli outsiders, dependent on each other and helping each other in this big, unfamiliar land. "One for all and All for one," they declared jokingly, but the sentiment was also heartfelt.

It was a much happier family that departed Philadelphia. They had experienced America and saw the incredible wealth and the equally incredible poverty, the openness and generosity, the greed and despair.

Then, Béla and Fanny and Rita found themselves back in Rehovot, in their old life that was somehow new with an expanded family and a greater appreciation of what Israeli life offered them.

Béla settled back into his work at Brown Furs. Of the three of them, he was the most changed, no longer the brooding, regretful person he had been for too many years. He had regained his self-confidence and optimism in Philadelphia and he was again gregarious and charming. He was determined that he would work even harder, relish his wife and daughter and, perhaps, even start his own business. Why not? He had launched a business in Bucharest, he had launched a business in America, albeit for others, why not try the same thing in Israel? Yes, why not?

And that was what he set out to do.

Chapter Sixteen: Haunted by the Past

Dayn mazl, Got, vos du voynst azoy hoykh; anit volt men dir di fentster oysgezetst.
You're lucky, God, that you live so high; otherwise people would break your windows.
— Stutchkoff, Der Oytser fun der Yidisher Shprakh.

Béla was by nature gregarious and boisterous. He made friends easily, and generously offered to help and share with virtual strangers what limited resources he could squirrel away from Fanny's grip over the family's finances. Fanny told Béla that he was too trusting, too naïve, an easy target for people to take advantage of him, and she was especially dismayed when, in social settings, she would overhear Béla boast about good turns in the family's fortune.

"Fanny doesn't like that I have a big mouth. But I have nothing to hide," he would exclaim when he noticed Fanny's disapproving look. Then, laughing, he would add, with relish: "Rita is just like me. She got the mouth from her father, but the brain from her mother." In time, Rita would acknowledge that there was some truth in this observation, and decided it would make an apt epitaph on her headstone.

Both Fanny and Rita also continued to feel acutely embarrassed by Béla whenever he was conversing with people in Hebrew. Béla felt no inhibition about his limited command of the language, which was actually not so limited in the vocabulary used in ordinary conversation, but lacked knowledge of correct grammar. Béla read voraciously the daily Israeli newspapers (*Maariv* or *Yedyot Aharonot* or *HaAretz*) and he listened earnestly to news broadcasts on the radio, but lacking formal education beyond the sixth grade and lacking the opportunities that Fanny and Rita had to learn Hebrew in a structured setting, his verbal communications lacked refinement.

Fanny and Rita were also uneasy when, in polite company, they would overhear Béla passionately espouse his critical views of Israeli politics or politicians, and his notions of how world leaders should conduct international affairs. Béla was informed about current events, he held strong opinions, and was not shy about expressing them. Yet these attributes didn't earn him credit with Fanny or Rita. In their critical eyes, he was a stubborn man with simple ideas and lacking subtlety in social manners. In their eyes, he was too direct, too honest and too loud. Compared to him, they were quieter, more introverted and introspective.

Béla sensed their annoyance and he withdrew emotionally.

The spell that had kept the family glued in Philadelphia dissolved when Béla, Fanny, and Rita resumed their old life in Rehovot and Tel Aviv. Their emotional closeness in the US was spurred by their common experience of being foreigners in a new land. The new friendships that the Izsáks made in America—with Béla's employers, with neighbors, acquaintances and colleagues of Fanny's from work, created lively, interesting experiences that enveloped them with good feelings.

They also enjoyed exciting shopping sprees in Philadelphia and New York City, choosing from a vast selection the appliances and gadgets to buy and ship to their home back in Israel. They bought large appliances—a refrigerator, a gas range with oven, a washing machine, a record player and a television (even though Israel had no TV broadcasts at the time). They also bought smaller appliances—a toaster, Minolta camera, transistor radios, and even a hair dryer—rare luxuries in Israel of that period.

After the gratifying year in Philadelphia, when they were back in Rehovot, the family again settled into a rhythm of 'live and let live,' each of them immersed in their own interests and activities with little overlap. Fanny happily returned to her work at the Weizmann. She was glad to resume the pleasant social contacts with her old colleagues and friends and she enjoyed visiting her siblings who were now accessible although scattered in Jerusalem, Caesaria, and Ramat-Gan. She liked to travel with Rita to concerts and theaters in Tel Aviv, and she relished reading together with Rita books that were required for Rita's school work, and going to the public library to check out more books for leisure reading.

Rita was similarly content with her life back home. She was back in high school to complete her senior year, and she was dating a handsome young man in uniform, Arie Schinnar, a lieutenant and tank commander in the Israeli army. The same 'boy' who would later fight in the Sinai campaign during the 1967 Six Days War and again in the Sinai campaign during the 1973 Yom Kippur War, and later, because of this military experience and his artistic talent, get accepted to the University of Texas A&M in College Station to study architecture. Eventually, he would also bring Rita back to America with him.

Béla, returned to his work at Brown Furs, but he was secretly contemplating the right time to start his own business, to be independent again, to be his own boss as he had been in Bucharest when he was first starting out at only 21.

Eventually, Béla opened Béla Furs on *Rehov Ben-Yehuda* in Tel Aviv—a street named after a remarkable man, Eliezer Ben-Yehuda, who was born in 1858, in what is now Bélarus, and who, more or less, single-handedly established the use of modern Hebrew as the language of everyday conversation in Israel. After emigrating to Palestine in 1881, Ben-Yehuda was motivated both by a passionate desire to make it possible for all the Jews of the Diaspora to communicate with each other in a common language and by his disdain for Yiddish, although it was the spoken language of his youth. He raised his son to be the first native-speaker of Hebrew. It is said that he screamed at his wife when he heard her singing a Russian lullaby to the boy when he was still a baby. It is somewhat ironic that Béla opened his shop on a street named after the man who created modern Hebrew, since Béla himself never became truly fluent in the language.

When Béla opened his shop, *Rehov Ben-Yehuda* was already an elegant commercial boulevard that ran from south to north starting from *Rehov Allenby* in the south, with the Mediterranean sea wall to the west, then running parallel to *Rehov Disengoff* which it then joined in the north at Yarkon Park, Tel Aviv's largest park with its gardens, sports facilities, concert venues and lakes. As a result, Béla's shop was well located to capture any foot traffic walking past his display window where mannequins were dressed in his artful fur coats and jackets. However, the heart of the shop was reached through a narrow alley that ran alongside his display window. The alley then opened up into two simple rooms.

The front room was modestly decorated with a coffee table, a few upholstered armchairs, viewing mirrors and racks of coats and jackets in different styles and types of furs (mink, chinchilla, nutria, sable, silver fox). The back room was where the worktables, supplies and unfinished furs were stored and where the seamstresses and assistants labored, their numbers growing or shrinking at different times, depending on the workload.

At work, Béla wore a white coat over nicely pressed shirts and slacks, in the style of medical professionals. "The clothes make the person," he would say and, no matter what he was feeling inside, he also always wore a huge smile and twinkling eyes for the customers.

For the modest establishment that it was, Béla Furs was a successful business. It soon also established a reputation as a place where many of the people who worked on or near *Rehov Ben-Yehuda* liked to hang out. Mostly they were furrier friends, like Motl', his former boss at Brown Furs, or Smuk, Misha and Lotzi—Hungarian owners of their own fur stores, or Beneşi, Victor and Zoli—Romanians who worked in those stores, who just wanted to chat about old times or to trade pelts, finished products or tools. Then, there were the hangers-on: other merchants, vendors, salesmen, even street artists from whom Béla would sometimes buy oil paintings, and the occasional prostitute—people that simply enjoyed the free-flowing atmosphere at the back of the shop, where they often took advantage of Béla's generosity and his extroverted spirit.

The hard work (for Béla was, as always, a dedicated, hard worker and even more so when he was in business for himself) and the difficult daily commute between Rehovot and Tel Aviv left Béla with little free time to spend at home with Fanny and Rita. The commute required Béla to walk a significant distance from their house on *Rehov Mohliver* to *Rehove HaRashi* (Main Street) to pick up a bus to get to the central terminal near the bustling *Shuk HaCarmel* (Carmel Market) in Tel Aviv. From there he had to walk over to get a second bus to reach his store on *Rehov Ben-Yehuda*.

At the Tel Aviv bus terminal it was common to encounter large crowds pushing their way, trying to be first to board the bus, hoping to get a seat or even standing room. A full bus would move on, and those unlucky not to board it, had to wait until the next bus arrived. It was tiring to wait and tiring to hassle with an impatient, hot-tempered crowd. And the bus ride was long. Sometimes, when Béla worked late or he was too tired, he would reluctantly take a taxi home to Rehovot, which was expensive but faster and easier on the spirit. Regardless of the hardship, Béla dutifully came home. He would eat the meal that Fanny prepared for him, then take a shower, then retire to bed.

Fanny did not enjoy going to Béla's shop because she felt uncomfortable among his workers and friends who were speaking Hungarian, a language that she did not try to learn. Fanny was also displeased to see the assortment of visitors that stopped by for casual chatting. She thought these people were interfering with Béla's work and their loud presence possibly turning away clients.

Despite her long-simmering dissatisfaction in the marriage, it was difficult for Fanny to consider breaking off with Béla. Her own Old World upbringing did not put a premium on love as a foundation for marriage. She was also reluctant to break up the relationship, fearing it would harm Rita. And she still felt continuing affection for her charming rascal of a husband. However, the prophesy that her Uncle Sami once made that, over time, during their married life, "Fanny would grow a little older next to Béla, and Béla would grow a little younger next to Fanny," and their ages would not be a source of friction and misunderstanding between them, was a prophecy that didn't quite work out. Of course, it was not just their ages, but also the differences in their personalities, experiences, and interests. However, the union stood fast, although it was not always easy for either of them.

One warm summer evening, when a few friends and employees in Béla's shop were throwing a pre-birthday party for Béla, a party separate from the formal party that Fanny was planning with their extended families, the drinks were flowing and there were couples dancing in the workroom. Simcha, a temporary worker in Béla's shop from Turkey was flirting with the young seamstress from Russia, and Ziggy, the Hungarian worker from the fur store across the street, was having a friendly argument with Béla about the relative merits of Siberian silver fox versus Scandinavian blue fox, when a middle-aged woman wandered into the party. She was rather plain in appearance and her unfashionable dress added nothing to her appearance. She would have been altogether unremarkable except for the fact that she kept staring at Béla.

Finally Ziggy asked Béla, "Do you know that woman?"

"What woman?" answered Béla.

"That woman," said Ziggy as he pointed across the room toward the woman who continued to stare at Béla. Béla glanced over his shoulder and then turned back to Ziggy. "No, why?"

"She keeps staring at you."

"Don't they all?" Béla joked.

Ziggy shrugged. "She's just…well, a little strange. Looks very tense. Not smiling at all."

"She's only a stranger who happened upon our party," said Béla. "She'll probably leave soon enough."

But the woman didn't leave. She continued to focus on Béla and after awhile she was making Béla nervous, so he walked over to speak to her.

"Why do you keep looking at me?" he asked.

She answered in Romanian: "You don't remember me?"

Béla was disconcerted. Something about her voice stirred a deep response.

"Blood-red and snow-white roses. Candlelight. A gypsy violinist playing Bartók. Do you remember these?" she asked.

Béla blanched and staggered backwards as if he were seeing a ghost, which in fact he was.

"*Dumnezeule meu!* (My God)," he exclaimed in Romanian. "Sárika?" he sputtered. "But…but…you're…"

"Yes. You left me there to die."

Béla threw up his hands. "No," he yelled, "No…"

"But I didn't die, Béla."

Béla struggled to breath. Simcha heard the commotion and rushed to his side. "What's wrong, Béla?"

Béla couldn't answer him. He felt as if he would collapse when Ziggy appeared at his other elbow and held Béla upright.

"It must be nice to have so many friends," said Sári, somewhat bitterly.

"Why is she speaking to you in Romanian?" said Ziggy.

Béla finally managed to pull himself together, but only barely. "An old friend," he gasped.

"Friend?" said Sári. She slapped him hard across his left cheek as 25 years of anger, fear, loneliness and pain exploded from inside her. "Friend?" she repeated in her rage.

Simcha tried to restrain Sári while Ziggy propped up Béla. "Leave her alone," said Béla, "please, please leave her alone," he said to Simcha.

Then to Sári, "Come with me…we…I…" There were tears in his eyes, but not from her slap.

They walked together down *Shderot Ben-Gurion*, across *Rehov Ha-Yarkon*, to the sea wall, just below the marina where they sat and talked until dawn. Sári apologized for her outburst and explained that she hadn't been looking for him all those years, but when she saw the sign above the display window of his shop, she realized she had to find out if it was her Béla from long ago. Then her emotions just took over.

Béla told her about the closed border and the fact that he couldn't get back into Transylvania to rescue her or his family. He told her that he spoke to Daitel Mișu in Bucharest after the war and Daitel told Béla that Sári and Béla's mother Stefánia, and his little brother Yaakov had all died in Auschwitz. For a moment there on the sea wall, Béla briefly hoped that perhaps Stefánia and Yaakov were also alive, but Sári told him that what Daitel said about his mother and brother was correct—that they were truly dead.

He asked her how they died. She said he didn't want to know that. He asked her about Auschwitz and she said he didn't want to know about that either. He asked her how she survived and she told him he really didn't want to know about that. She explained that she eventually made her way back to Bucharest after she was released from a Displaced Persons camp, only to find out that Béla had remarried and left with his new family for Israel. She decided that he was dead to her and she forced herself to banish all memory of him from her mind. Then, recently, she was also allowed to emigrate to Israel and she was trying to adapt to the country, but she was having a rough time of it.

He asked her where she wanted to live. "America," she said, "or maybe, Canada. But then I have a friend who went to Mexico. She likes it there." She paused for a moment, dreaming. "Maybe Paris. I always wanted to go to Paris."

"Maybe I can help you," Béla exclaimed.

As the sun rose over the city behind them and they were both staring out at the gentle waves from the Mediterranean lapping against the shore, each was thinking about the strange twists of life they had both, in there own way, experienced. It was a difficult moment. Then Sári suddenly said, "It's time to go, Béla." He didn't try to dissuade her because he too had to get back home.

When he walked into the apartment in Rehovot, Fanny was furious. "A night with a 'special client'?" she said sarcastically.

At first, Béla didn't respond to Fanny's anger, but then he felt he had to say something about the overwhelming news. "She's alive," he said.

"Who's alive?"

"Sárika. My first wife. She came to the shop last night."

Fanny was stunned. "But she is dead."

"I thought so too. All these years, I was sure," said Béla.

"Did you sleep with her?" asked an incredulous and confused Fanny.

"Oh, God no, Fanny. It wasn't like that at all."

Fanny couldn't help herself. She started to cry. "What are you going to do?"

"I don't know," said Béla. "I really don't know."

Needless to say, Béla's second birthday party in Rehovot with his extended family was a somber affair although neither Béla nor Fanny told anyone about Sári. Not that night, nor at any other time.

For weeks Béla walked around in a daze, absorbing the news about Sári, and re-experiencing the pain of losing his mother and brother under such horrible circumstances. He sent away the hangers-on who frequented his shop. Fanny had the good sense to allow Béla to grieve and come to terms with his loss and survivor guilt. Eventually, Béla concluded he had to do something and he came up with a plan.

He went to the bank and withdrew all of his savings from his Béla Furs business account. He then tracked down Sári through the Jewish Agency for Israel and they met in a small café on the eastern edge of Tel Aviv where they were not likely to be recognized. Béla was trembling as he handed Sári a large manila envelope. "It's in dollars," he said. "Go wherever your dreams take you."

"I don't want your guilt money, Béla." She shoved the envelope back across the small table.

"I thought you might say that," said Béla, "but it's not guilt money, Sárika. Really it's not. I thought about what happened and I still don't see what else I could have done. It was the war. That terrible war. Those terrible times. What terrible people did to all of us, the living and the dead."

Sári sat silently.

"There's nothing I can do for my mother or my brother, but I can do this for you. Please take the money and use it to make your life what you want it to be."

Sári considered what Béla said. Then she stood and took the envelope. She leaned down and kissed Béla chastely on the cheek where she had slapped him. "I can't give you a real kiss," she said, "the pain is still too strong. But I can thank you for your generosity and to apologize for slapping you."

Béla nodded. "I'm glad you survived, Sári. I hope you can make a new life."

Sári turned away. She may have been crying when she left the café, but she didn't say anything and she didn't turn back toward Béla.

For the next year, Béla worked even harder than he normally did. He wanted to replenish the money he had given to Sári, money that rightly was also Fanny's, and he wanted to prove to himself that by doing all the right things, he deserved to have survived the war and become relatively prosperous.

He continued to smile for all his customers, but those close to him saw a sadness and emotional exhaustion. One day in his workshop, he was pushing hard to finish two mink jackets for an important client, a local businessman who brought his two business partners from overseas to Béla, to place the orders as gifts to take back to their wives. He carelessly lifted himself up much too quickly from under one of the sinks where he had stored a box of supplies, and he severely slammed his skull against the unyielding cast iron. He immediately saw stars and sat down on the floor trying to recover. After some time, he thought he was going to be all right and paid no more attention to this incident.

He continued his daily trips to Tel Aviv, and continued to work furiously, until late one evening, about six weeks after he hit his head, a neighbor found him collapsed in a heap on the floor at the doorstep of the house. Béla had made it back to Rehovot from Tel Aviv at the end of a long day in the store, and he managed to walk the distance from where the taxi driver had dropped him off to the house, but before reaching for his key to open the door or before ringing the doorbell, he crumbled to the ground.

The neighbor called for an ambulance even before knocking on the door to inform Fanny. When they took Béla to the emergency room at the Kaplan Medical Center, it was touch and go whether Béla would make it through the night. His condition was serious enough to require immediate transfer to the larger and better-equipped Beilinson Hospital in *Petach Tikva* (Gate of Hope, as this town, coincidentally is named) about 40 kilometers north of Rehovot. Neurological test results showed that Béla had a severe hematoma, and the swelling in his cranium required surgery to drain the blood from between his brain and skull because the excess blood was creating dangerous pressure on his cerebellum.

Once that operation was successful and the immediate danger had passed, there was concern about whether there had been any permanent damage to

Béla's brain. He was in a coma and it was uncertain if he would come out of his stupor or remain unconscious, perhaps forever.

Rita, who by this time was married and was abroad with her husband, was urged by Fanny to return home. Days passed. Fanny and Rita sat at Béla's bedside, talking to him, telling him stories, chatting in Romanian and sometimes even in Yiddish which they preferred not to speak, anything to try and bring Béla out from under his comatose state. Béla's brothers and some friends stopped by the hospital to talk with the unresponsive Béla, hoping their efforts would stimulate some reaction. Was Béla hearing them? Did he even want to come back to the hellish anguish since Sárika reappeared in his life? Was he done punishing himself?

One morning, Béla opened his eyes and saw the early morning light shining through his window on the face of his Fanny who had fallen asleep in her chair near his hospital bed. He had been dreaming about his mother and his childhood in Gâlgău when he ran in the woods with his friends and picked wild berries to bring home to Stefánia.

Béla blinked once, twice. He studied Fanny's peaceful face and realized he was still alive, in a hospital, in Israel. His thoughts were foggy at first, but slowly a clarity followed. Something was different. He was the same man. He felt all of the inner strength and hope and desire he had always felt, but the anxiety was gone, the fear was gone. He felt no need to prove anything and his heart was filled with the simple joy and excitement of being alive.

"Oh God, what things didn't I experience in this life already?" he thought to himself, amazed that he somehow came through so many challenging trials.

In the following weeks and months, as he slowly recovered, he found that he had developed an insatiable desire to see the beauty in things, and he wanted to appreciate his friends and family in deeper, less judgmental ways. In the years to come, Fanny and Rita often joked between themselves that his accident had given them a "new and improved Béla" and, truth be told, if Béla had heard them talking like that, he would have agreed with them. He felt that he was a better man and he vowed to live the rest of his life in a kinder, more gentle way.

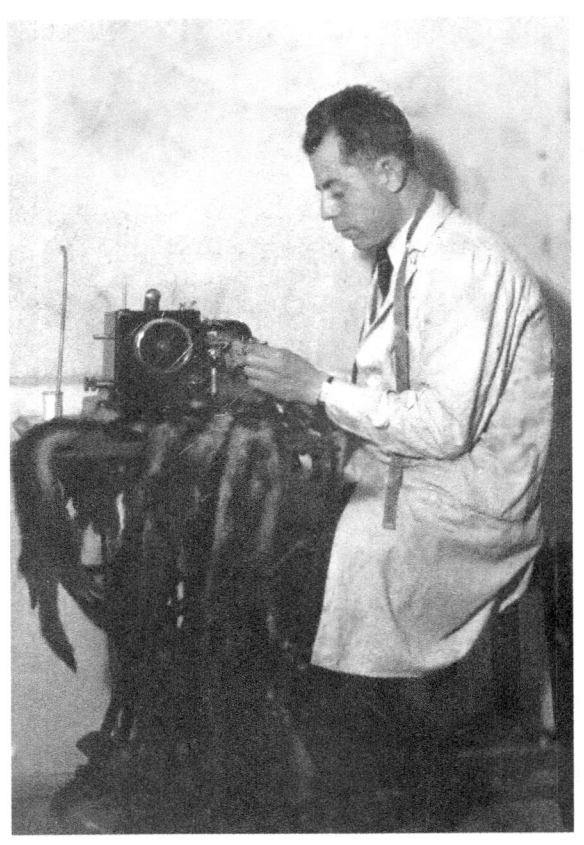

(above) Business card for Béla Furs in 1966.

Béla working at what he loved most—handling furs. (right) On the sewing machine with luxuriant fur pelts. (below) Designing a fur coat.

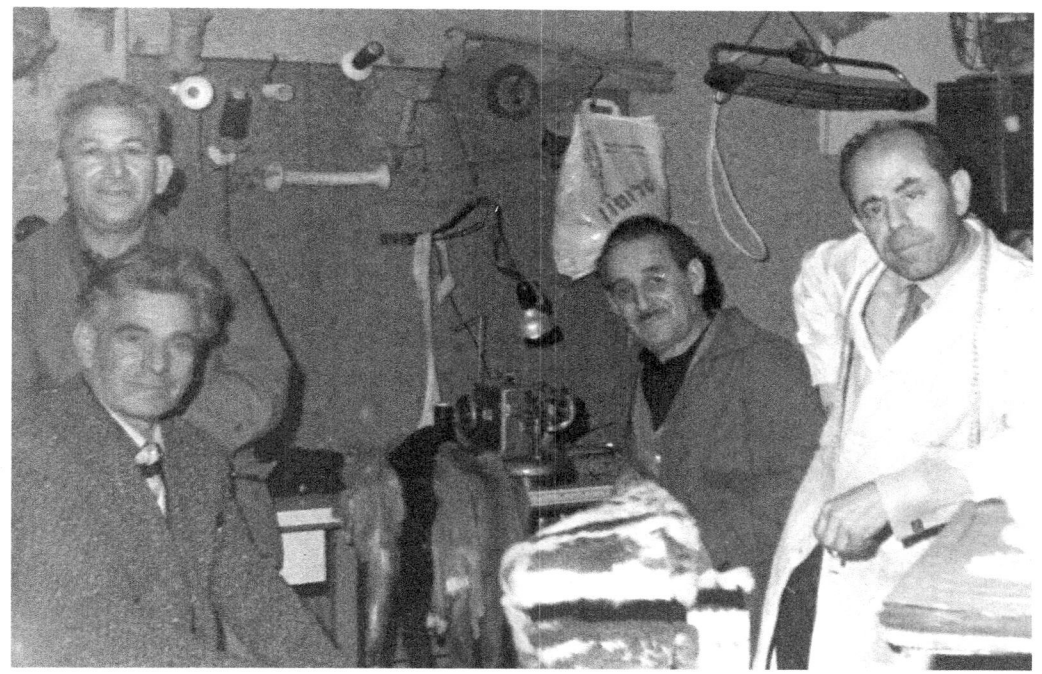

(above) Béla with a few of the workers in his shop.

(right and below) Totally at ease in his element: Béla wearing a white coat over pressed slacks, surrounded by fur jackets and coats that he designed in the modest showroom of Béla Furs in Tel Aviv, Israel, in the early 1970s.

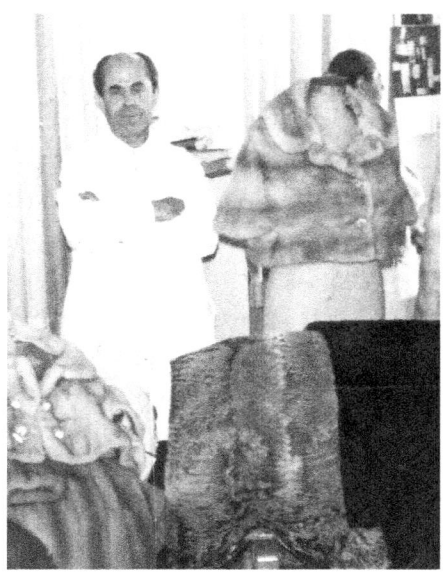

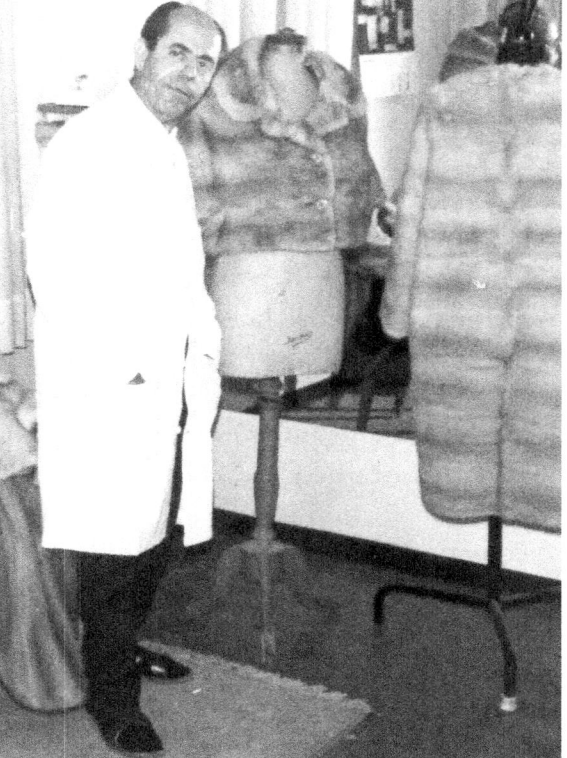

Chapter Seventeen: The Correspondence

Vi kumt di kats ibern vaser?
How does a cat cross over the water?
— Bernstein, Jüdische Sprichwörter und Redensarten.

Béla's recovery was not easy. Although he was miraculously free from any confused speech, further loss of consciousness or bouts of confusion—symptoms that often accompany a subdural hematoma, he did experience difficulty with his balance, serious trouble walking and a general lack of strength. These were understandable effects of his accident and surgery. After all, Béla was 63 years old although he did not appear that old nor did he act as if he were near retirement, which, in fact, he was not, and he would continue to work for the next 21 years.

He was a stubborn man. Even in his sadly helpless condition, he refused to be transferred to a rehab facility and he resolutely rejected a wheelchair. He was adamant in his wish to be sent home, where he would devise exercises for himself to strengthen his legs and the muscles in his arms.

Rita stayed with Béla to help him get stronger and, in doing so, she sacrificed time away from her studies and away from her husband who remained in the US. Gradually, Béla taught himself to stand up, then to take a few steps holding unto a cane. Then he forced himself to leave the house to go outside just to the small garden in from of the house, and after a while to walk a bit further to a nearby park where he would sit on a bench in the sun. Then he shed the cane and, before long, he was like his old self again, walking in his customary rushed pace. And then, he was back at his shop, making the hard commute daily between Rehovot and Tel Aviv, without anyone helping him. Years later, he would show the same determination and miraculous ability to bounce back when challenged by another curve ball.

Although Béla was completely recovered and delighted to be back working in his shop, he found that he was uncharacteristically lonely and, at first, he couldn't figure out why he was feeling that way. Gradually, he came to realize that he had grown very close to Rita while she was helping him with his rehabilitation and he missed her.

On one of his commutes from the central bus terminal in Tel Aviv to his shop, as he was randomly gazing out the bus window at the various elegant shops lining *Rehov Dizengoff*, he saw a stationary store, which reminded him that he needed to buy a new ledger for his business accounts, which triggered the thought that he could start corresponding with Rita. He would share with her stories about parts of his early life that he had kept to himself, and he would open-up about his feelings that he had kept inside and was not comfortable talking about with either Fanny or Rita.

That evening back in Rehovot, when he sat down to compose the first letter, he was overcome with anxiety. What words would he use to express his feelings? What would Rita think when she read his letter? Would she write back and share her thoughts as well? Eventually he faced the question of what language he would use. Rita didn't know Hungarian and she preferred not to use Yiddish. He remained uncomfortable in Hebrew, so he chose Romanian and in making that choice, he picked up his pen and wrote: *Fiica mea dragă, Rita,* (My darling daughter, Rita…), and after that introduction, the words simply flowed out of him without his needing to stop and think about what he was writing.

He wrote about his childhood growing up in Gálgau. He wrote about losing his father when he was barely six years old and having no memory at all of this man. He wrote how his widowed mother worked to support her five young sons, and of the harsh choice she had to make, to interrupt their schooling and send them away, one after another, to learn a trade. He wrote how his youngest brother, the sixth son that his mother had from a second marriage, had it easier because he had a father to provide support, but how, in the end, this good fortune didn't do any good, because the young man and his father were both killed in the Holocaust.

He wrote how much he loved his mother and relied on her for advice and how, even as an adult, he missed her deeply. He wrote how he struggled to stay alive during the war years. He wrote about his moment of extreme despair that almost caused him to kill himself, before he was saved by a stranger. He wrote about how he came to meet Fanny in Bucharest and how uneasy he had felt at first, when he learned that she was only seventeen years old. He wrote about life in Bucharest immediately after World War II, his successful business, the luxurious apartment that he and Fanny had lived in, how excited they were when Rita was born, how wonderful life was for those few brief years. He was a successful man, a proud father, and the husband to a lovely young wife. He also wrote that even then, he was consumed by work and spent little time at home with his new daughter and that he now felt badly that he hadn't taken the time to truly appreciate the miracle of his little girl.

He wrote about his dread when he realized that the post-war peace had not really changed anti-Semitic attitudes in Romania and, to make matters worse, the rise of the Communists destroyed the entrepreneurial success he had worked so hard to build. He explained that he needed to move his young family out of Bucharest to the safety of Israel, leaving behind family and friends and whatever wealth and comfort he had attained, and arriving in Israel with nothing other than their high hopes and expectations and his conviction that they would soon be living well in their new paradise.

Then he acknowledged that from the very beginning of their life in Rehovot, despite his outward optimism and determination, he felt humiliated, inadequate and frustrated. He never minded hard work, but he hated roofing houses. It was grueling work in the hot sun, inhaling tar odor, and causing his hands to swell with painful blisters. He despised the unruly horses and the unwilling mules that he kept to pull his rickety old wagon that he used to deliver ice blocks. He begrudged the backbreaking task of transporting the ice blocks to customers who treated him worse than they would the lowest common laborer. He was proud of Fanny's accomplishments, but he felt he was an inadequate husband because he was stuck in menial jobs. He confessed that those feelings often made him sullen and remote.

> I'm telling you, Rita, I expected to encounter a few hurdles in my life, being that I was born in a small village in Hungary, being that I was born a Jew, being that from the age of six years old I had no father and my poor mother had to raise five small boys on her own. But in my wildest dreams I would not have expected to ride the adventurous road that fate laid out for me. When I think of all the things that had happened to me and all the things that I did in my life, even I can't believe that it was I who experienced these things. I was not always wise. I did not behave well. But often I didn't know any better.

He also told Rita how happy he had been when the family had picnicked together on the coastal beaches at *Rishon LeZion* or *Bat-Yam*, when he carried little Rita on his shoulders as he swam across the lagoon to *Ha-Sella*, and how her excitement and delight on those wonderful days together almost convinced him that the hard times were worth it. He wanted Rita to understand that was the way things were back then.

> I could have been a better husband and a better father, but only

lately I figured out that the 'tone makes the music,' so to speak… If I had tried to be more patient, more attentive, more thoughtful, things might have been different. But as the saying goes, better late than never… I hope it's not too late for us.

Being painfully aware of Rita's insecurities, despite of her outgoing personality, and worried that he might have contributed to these, Béla felt compelled to say more.

Believe me, you are beautiful and you are smart. You can do anything. I was always proud of you. You were a little girl with a nice singing voice and I went to talk with the Director of Kol Israel [Israel's public radio broadcast service] and I asked him to let you sing on the radio. I really believed that you had talent. Unfortunately, he turned me down. He laughed and said that all parents think their kids have great talent… But I tried. At least I have always enjoyed listening to you when you sang the opera arias or popular Israeli songs on our balconies at home. And I especially loved when you sang to me Bartók's 'Songs That My Mother Taught Me.'

When I slapped your face once, when I came home from work and saw you with your friends and you were biting your fingernails, I did this out of love. I wanted to teach you, once and for all, to stop biting your fingernails. I wasn't thinking of your friends and the humiliation that you might feel. I was upset that you were ten years old and still were biting your nails.

When I hit you once, but only once, with my belt, when you were very little, when we still lived in the tent, I did it because you stole one lira [Israeli paper currency equivalent to a one dollar bill]. One lira at that time in Israel was worth a fortune and you took the money and went out to buy buckets of popcorn to share with all your little friends in tent city. But I hit you to teach you that stealing was really a very bad thing to do.

And when I shouted on you during your teens to convince you, against your will, to join your mother and me on the trips to visit our old relatives—Nenea Sami and Tanti Betty, Nenea Matei and the other Tanti Betty, Nenea Itzik and Tanti Klara— I did it to teach you the importance of respect for elders. They had no one in Israel except us and we owed it to them to know that we cared.

I know that you learned all those lessons, and I know that you never forgave me for how I behaved, but I didn't know how to teach you these things differently. Nothing in my past taught me how to be a good father. I acted on impulse. I did it the *dugree* way [the blunt Israeli way of speaking and acting]. I did it from the heart, not from the head. I loved you and wanted you to be the best.

When Rita received the thick letter from Israel with Béla's hand-writing on the front, she was intrigued because Béla had never written to her before.

At first, she was startled by how beautifully he wrote and expressed his feelings. He embellished the nouns with colorful adjectives and he used the verbs and adverbs imaginatively. He sprinkled his letter with Romanian expressions and even with some Hebrew expressions that were funny and poignant. He wrote penetratingly and with sensitivity about what he had been through in life. This was not the father she had come to accept over the years. She cried, tears streaming down her cheeks, when she read about Béla's deep-held pain and frustration and anger. Then she realized that the letter was her father's apology for not being the attentive father she had wanted him to be when she was a little girl.

Rita wrote back to Béla in Romanian since it was clearly the language that allowed her father to communicate his deepest emotions. She told him that she had always admired his boundless energy and apparent optimism, but she was often hurt when he seemed to ignore her or harshly correct her when she fell short of his standards, that she perceived to be conservative and old-fashioned. She agreed that she also had wonderful memories of their Saturdays at the beach or watching him at his worktable behind the stables apartment. She remembered how thrilled she had been when he allowed her to help him work on a fur collar and how good she felt when he complimented her when she sang, and for playing the accordion while he sang along with her, although she had to include the teasing rebuke and reminder that she actually hated the accordion.

And then Rita dug deeper into her feelings. She told Béla the truth: that during her childhood she was often embarrassed by his appearance in his filthy work clothes when he was delivering ice blocks to the homes of her playmates and classmates. She was humiliated in front of her friends when Béla spoke his faltering, inadequate Hebrew. She admitted that she hated many of the stupid presents he brought her because they didn't seem to have anything to do with what she wanted and, thus, made her feel like her father wasn't really listening to her. And she confessed that for many years she had carried a bitterness inside her for the 'brutish' way in which he taught her to tell the good from the bad.

Then she wrote about how her feelings began to change when the family spent their year together in Philadelphia. She enjoyed helping him adapt to life in the United States, and appreciated his willingness to let her help him. She saw that many of the adults who were the Izsák's friends in America really liked her father, and she understood that people like the Wengers truly appreciated and valued his skills as a furrier. She came to enjoy the family's various trips and daily excursions when she experienced Béla's enthusiasm and curiosity as genuine emotions. And as she wrote about those times, she realized that the change came about when she learned to respect her father when she saw him through the eyes of Americans.

She wrote about how terrified she was that she would lose him when he was in a coma, and how much she admired him as he struggled to overcome the effects of his accident and his surgery. Rita told him that it was during his recovery that she finally understood his inner strength and determination, his unwavering commitment not to give up hope that things would get better. And then, when she received the letter he had written her, his words helped her understand that his determination to never give up was how he coped with the terrible disappointments in his life. Then, she told him she loved him.

When Rita's letter arrived in Rehovot, Béla couldn't wait to open it, but he was also afraid to read what she would say to him. He let the letter sit on the kitchen counter until Fanny laughed and told him that if he didn't open it, she would open it, so Béla picked up the letter and went out onto the balcony as he read.

When he walked back into the apartment, he had a big smile on his face. He grabbed Fanny and started to dance with her, although the only music he heard was coming from inside his heart and not from any outside source.

Fanny was delighted to see Béla so rambunctious and happy. "So tell me what she wrote you about life in the US," said Fanny.

"She didn't write about her life in the US," said Béla, "she wrote about how she felt about me. She says she loves me after all," Béla joked.

Béla gave Rita's letter to Fanny and Fanny read what Rita said to Béla. When she finished reading, she said: "It's true. You really did get your confidence back when we were in Philadelphia."

"Yes," replied Béla, "I got my confidence when I finally made it to America. When I met civilized people that didn't hate me, like Madam Traivish used to and showed it each time when I crossed the old courtyard with the horse and the wagon. When I met civilized people who didn't hit me over the head with a dirty shoe, like some of the Moroccan and Tunisian and Iraqi clients used to do whenever I ran out of ice blocks to deliver to their shacks. When I finally met civilized people that didn't come after me with sticks and stones, like our Yemenite neighbors who were angry that my wild horse toppled their outhouses and trampled over their gardens. When I met civilized people that didn't scream or push me so they could get in front of me at the long line at the bus terminal in Tel Aviv. Of course my confidence returned when the Wengers appreciated my skills and showered me with compliments and love. America was the antidote to my years of misery in the first years as a newcomer in Israel."

"They did, Béla. But people here like you too. You have so many furrier friends in Tel Aviv now. And you have your family here, your brothers from Romania."

"But not Rita. Rita is in America."

As Fanny gently reminded Béla about how wonderful their life was in Israel and that Béla should be content because he was his own boss in his fur business that was doing well, she was also wrestling with a gnawing understanding that, for some reason she didn't fully comprehend, both her husband and her daughter found life in America more compatible than life in Rehovot.

That night, Béla composed a second letter to Rita in which he tried to fully explain the guilt he experienced when he inadvertently abandoned his mother, and his first wife, a woman named Sárika, in Hungarian-controlled Transylvania, how he could not get back to save them and, then, his total devastation when he realized they had been rounded up by the Nazis and shipped off to Germany, while he was free to live and work in Bucharest. And, finally, his complete collapse when he found out that they had been murdered in the concentration camp at Auschwitz.

> I am telling you, Rita, I have lived with my private pain and guilt and shame for many years. I sometimes wake up at night and I lie awake, very still in bed so not to wake up your mother, and I think about life. Life is like a thin thread that can easily snap.
>
> How could I have known when I left Galgau in 1944 that one part of my life would come to an end, so abruptly and so tragically? Even today I miss my mother. I really loved her and I always respected her advice.

He wrote about how he fell in love with the beautiful young Fanny and how he rebuilt his life, only to have it threatened by the Communists when they came to power and his subsequent determination not to let others take everything away from him yet again.

He did his best to explain how humiliated he had felt during those early days in Israel, and that he knew both Fanny and Rita were disappointed that he was unable to adapt to their new life as easily as they were. He told her how he had developed a fantasy that if he could only make it to America, then he would be happy again and he would make things better for Rita and Fanny, but he failed in his scheme to accomplish that, as well.

> Nothing comes easy in life. Nothing in this life is handed to you on a platter. A person must take risks, must try out things and if they don't work out, at least he is left with some experience. Only the persons who expect little in life, have few disappointments. I had hopes, I took risks, I got my share of disappointments…

Then, as he sat there in the middle of the night debating whether he would tell her his deepest secret or not, he decided he would tell her how Sári had reappeared in Tel Aviv, that she had not been killed after all, and how seeing her and hearing again about what had happened to his mother had sent him into another emotional tailspin that eventually led to his accident in the shop.

> I sometimes think that maybe I was not correct with my first wife Sárika. I sent her away when she found me in Israel. I gave her money to go start a new life somewhere, but I can't help thinking that maybe the help was not enough or maybe I should have done something else. What remains in life without honor? Only shame. But what else could I have done? Things were so complicated then. I was already remarried and I had you. I couldn't imagine other ways to deal with Sárika.
>
> I never talked about this before, so I don't know why I am writing to you about these things now. Maybe I want you to understand that people are more complicated than what they let known. People swallow many bad pills in life and I had my share of them but, like a man sick with a bad cold, I take solace in the knowledge that things could have been worse. A sick man lives with pessimism; a healthy man lives with hope. I have lived with both. And Rita, you should at least remember this, to live your own life with hope. Don't give up.

And he ended with his deepest, heartfelt thanks that Fanny and Rita had brought him back again to the point where he was now able to tell them how much he cared for them, and how fervently he hoped that he would have many years left to make up for the pain he had caused and the rift that they had all felt.

From that point on, Béla, in Israel, and Rita, in America, continued their correspondence, and as they shared their deepest thoughts and emotions, they grew even closer. And Fanny and Béla, together in Rehovot, also began to understand each other better, perhaps better than they ever had before.

One balmy evening, as they sat on their balcony enjoying the scent of orange blossoms in the air, Fanny turned to Béla and said, "You know, Béla, I've been thinking that we should go visit Rita and Arie in Texas."

They took one month off in August to travel to College Station, Texas, where Rita and her husband Arie were attending college. Then, an odd thing happened. Rita and Arie took Béla and Fanny on a touring trip to the Dallas-Fort Worth area. They were casually walking along an elegant street, window-shopping near the original flagship Neiman-Marcus store, when Béla suddenly disappeared. Stumped but not particularly concerned, Fanny, Rita and Arie continued to walk slowly and wander around the area, assuming that Béla would show up at some point, which he did.

"Béla, where have you been?" asked Fanny.

"I got a job," said Béla with a big grin on his face.

"*Tata*, what are you talking about?" said Rita.

"I stopped in that fur store that we passed over there," he pointed back down the block, "and they hired me to work for them."

"Just like that?" said Rita.

"No questions asked?" said Fanny.

Béla nodded.

"But you told them you couldn't take the job," said Fanny.

"No," said Béla. "I told them I would take the job."

"But...," said Rita.

"How...," said Fanny.

Béla was serious. He found a cheap place in a rooming house and he stayed behind in Dallas, while Rita, Arie and Fanny returned to College Station. When it was time to go back to Israel, Béla showed up in College Station, delighted with the unexpected money he had earned (albeit, earned illegally because he only had a tourist visa). He was also pleased with the updated techniques he'd learned in America and happy with the new friends he'd made in Texas.

On the plane going back to Israel, Fanny had a serious talk with Béla. "Things are not as good as they first appeared."

"What's the problem?"

"Rita may not be able to carry a child to term."

Béla shook his head. "But that's not possible," he said in total ignorance, "my mother had six children and your mother had four."

"Of course it's possible," said the more scientific and informed Fanny. "She's had two miscarriages already."

Béla was stunned. "What can we do?"

"We can't do anything, Béla. She's seeing a doctor. There's still hope."

But Béla continued to shake his head and refuse to believe that he would not have a grandchild who would be part of his family's legacy. As much as he tried to change and become a modern man, Béla was still caught up in some of the myths and prejudices of the Old World and, in those ways, he realized he might never change. However, at that point he was focused on his daughter's unhappiness and he could not have predicted what the future would bring for all of them during the many years he had left.

(above, left) Fanny in 1946, four months after being married at age 17. (above, right) Fanny in 1952 while still working as a sorter of Jaffa oranges for export. (below) Fanny (on the right) in 1960, taking classes and working at the Weizmann Institute of Science.

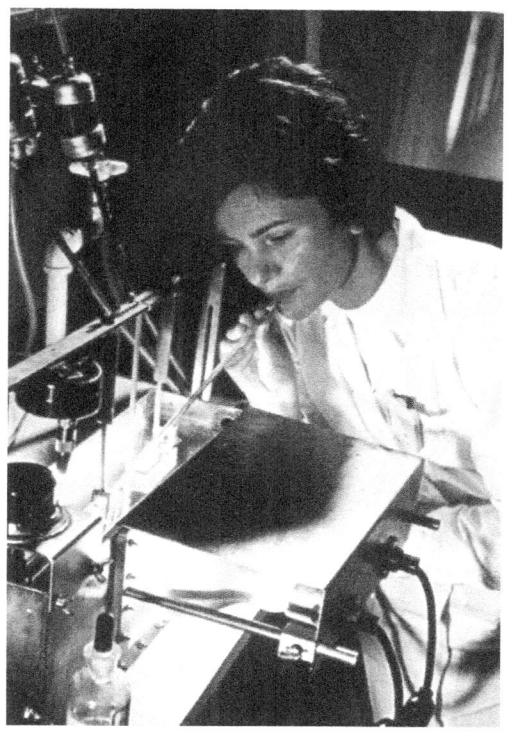
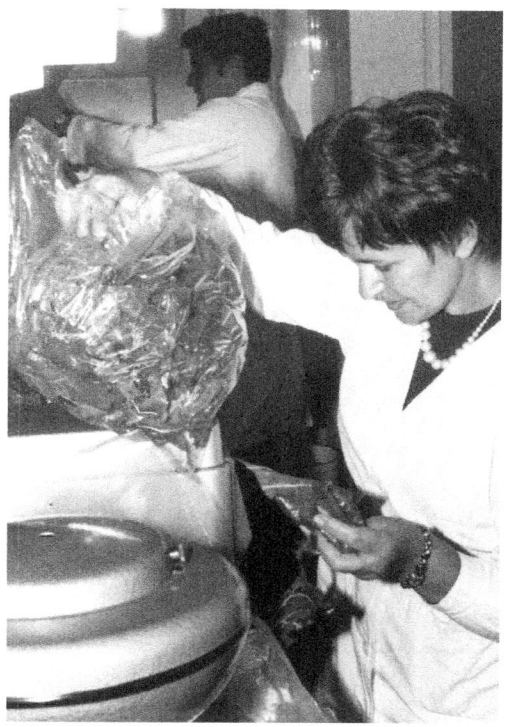

(above, left) Fanny in 1969, working on photosynthesis research at the Weizmann Institute.

(above, right) Fanny in 1971 at Brandies University, in Waltham, Mass. On the back of this picture that was addressed to Rita, she wrote: "A day when the entire team is working in the cold room. It is hard work, but the atmosphere is very jovial and pleasant."

(lower, right) Fanny in 2005, at her Philadelphia home, in retirement.

(above) Béla and Fanny together with Rita's in-laws, Mr. & Mrs. Rachel and Chaim Schmeidler, in Rehovot, Israel, in 1970. This picture was sent to Rita and Arie who were students in Texas at that time, to reassure them that all was well with the parents back home.

Béla and Fanny in front of their apartment in Waltham, Massachusetts in 1972, during a Sabbatical year when Fanny was working at Brandies University and Béla was working at Kakas Furs in Boston. They look happy here, so Nenea Sami's prediction, "Don't worry about the age difference. She'll grow older next to you...You'll grow younger next to her... With time you'll see the age difference go away...," came true.

(left) Béla and Fanny on a trip to Annapolis, Maryland in 1990, by now both were naturalized US citizens.

(below) Béla and Fanny in 2001, at Rita's wedding to Erling E Boe. Béla was 89, and walking with a cane after suffering a stroke two years earlier.

(left) Béla and Fanny in 2005, in front of their house in Philadelphia.

(left) Béla, Fanny and Rita in 1965, visiting the Liberty Bell in historic Philadelphia, during a Sabbatical year when Fanny was working at the University of Pennsylvania and Béla was working at Wenger Furs in Haddonfield, New Jersey.

(below) Béla and Rita in 1972, at her graduation from State University of New York at Buffalo.

(above) Fanny and Rita in 1972 at her graduation from State University of New York at Buffalo.

(left) Béla and Rita in 2006, at home in Philadelphia, just a few months before Béla passed away.

Chapter Eighteen: This Too Shall Pass

Di gantse velt iz eyn shtot.
The whole world is one town.
— Bernstein, Jüdische Sprichwörter und Redensarten.

After he and Fanny returned to Israel, Béla continued his emotional correspondence with Rita, but he eventually realized that writing to her was not as rewarding as seeing her, and he was unhappy that he could not spend more time with her. He wanted to help her cope with the stresses on her marriage, her ongoing attempts to build a career and her inability to carry a child to term, although he had to admit to himself that he had absolutely no idea whatsoever how he could possibly be helpful with any of those problems.

Béla did find, as he had when the family spent their first year in Philadelphia, that working with American furriers was exciting and challenging in ways that his work at his own shop in Tel Aviv was not. In Texas, he worked with advanced techniques for preparing pelts, technical equipment that aided precise cutting and measuring of the furs, and sewing machines that utilized early examples of computer-aided stitching. In Texas, designers were willing to experiment with the latest trends in contemporary fashion. Yes, his Old World skills of hands-on cutting and stretching and intense attention to detail were appreciated, but in America he not only learned new techniques, he also learned that the business was changing with the introduction of more realistic synthetic furs, because protests against wearing real fur were gaining strength.

These developments, plus the fact that Rita lived in the United States, pulled him toward wanting to live in America. But other countervailing arguments also had power over him: his surviving siblings were with him in Israel, he owned his own business in Israel, Fanny had a great job at the Weizmann Institute, and their home in the prime area of Rehovot was beautiful. Although his body was getting older on the outside, more visibly rounder compared to the bony skeleton that he was when he was delivering ice blocks, he was agile and his spirit was young and, despite his sincere and relatively successful effort to buckle down and appreciate his day-to-day life, he felt restless, envisioning more exciting challenges.

Then one evening, after harboring such thoughts for several years, Béla was sitting on the terrace in Rehovot after dinner, when Fanny presented him with her latest proposal. "Béla, Professor Avron again wants me to go with him to the United States."

Béla perked up. "Another year in America?"

"For me, yes, but what about you? Can you afford to abandon your business again for an entire year?"

Béla hesitated for, at most, a few seconds. "Yes, yes. Where are we going?"

"Brandeis University in Massachusetts. The university is in a small town called Waltham, but it appears to be just outside Boston. Maybe even a suburb."

"Rita's in Buffalo, New York," said Béla. "How near is Boston to Buffalo?"

"I looked at a map. We will be close, a lot closer than we are here, anyway."

So Béla closed Béla Furs, Fanny rented out the Rehovot apartment, and they were off to a new chapter of life in America. This time, the transition went much more smoothly. Fanny was confident in her work and had no trepidations about her ability to participate in research at Brandies. As to Béla, he and Rita once again meandered through unfamiliar streets, in Boston this time, looking for owners of fur establishments that would buy into the proposition that Béla, hailing from Hungary and Israel and possessing unique skills, would be a genuine asset to them. Almost immediately he found work at the very elegant furrier, Edward F. Kakas & Sons on Newbury Street, where Back Bay dowagers purchased their furs.

In the same year that Fanny and Béla were visiting and working in Boston, Rita was completing her undergraduate studies at the State University of New York at Buffalo and her husband was getting a Master's degree in Architecture. She had more miscarriages and they were not only affecting her health, they were contributing to increasing tension in her marriage. Although their studies kept Rita and Arie busy and shielded them from dealing with their problems, both Fanny and Béla sensed things were difficult for Rita. She often appeared despondent, which was uncharacteristic for her.

Béla's constant advice to Rita was that she needed to be more confident and hopeful. "You have the brain of a Golda Meir!" he would say to encourage her, invoking the image of the strong woman who was then Israel's prime minister. "You can do anything, be anyone, if only you believe in yourself." But these praises that Béla thought were so helpful only had the opposite effect by making

Rita even more convinced of her inadequacies which, in turn, contributed to her greater unhappiness.

Béla would have been surprised to find that his attempts to support Rita might not be working in the way he intended, because it had always been his own gregarious, confident nature that worked so well for him and that made him want to share his sense of hope and optimism with everyone he met. That part of his nature was always with him, even as he travelled back and forth each day between Waltham and Boston on the Fitchburg/South Acton commuter line. He spoke to anyone who happened to be seated next to him and within weeks he had developed new friends who enjoyed travelling with him and hearing his stories.

One day, a tall, slender, middle-aged man, dressed in the classic academic's muted plaid jacket with worn leather elbow patches and rumpled wool slacks, sat down next to Béla and set out to read the newspaper that he carried with him. When Béla glanced sideways and saw the headline news on the front page of the Wall Street Journal that the man was holding, news about President Nixon making a historic visit to the People's Republic of China, Béla took the initiative and spoke first. "Unbelievable! Anti-communist Nixon going to communist China?" he exclaimed. "Politics is very interesting," he added and, then, when another thought came to his mind, he shared that too: "I am sure this is from the big brain of Kissinger. His idea."

"Yes, politics is strange," concurred the tall man. Then, detecting the foreign accent, he turned to look at Béla and asked, "Where's your accent from?"

"It depends how far back you want to know," Béla answered coyly. "I was born in Hungary and I also lived in Romania and Israel." And then he added, "Hi. My name is Adalbert Izsák, but everybody calls me Béla. My wife works at Brandies."

The man was intrigued. "I work at Harvard University, but next year I am going with my family to Israel to work for a year at the Hebrew University of Jerusalem."

Béla was excited and genuinely curious. "What do you teach?"

"Economics."

"Ah, you know how to make money," Béla said.

The professor pressed his fingers to his forehead. "No, I just talk about it."

As the train jostled on the old track headed for Boston, Béla and the tall man learned more about each other.

"I always wanted to make a lot of money," said Béla. "I wanted a big car like the one I had before the war, and a big house with a big yard…"

"Before the war?"

"World War II. My mother and my brother were killed in Auschwitz. I lost my wife too. I thought I did. She came back to me. In Tel Aviv. Then she went away again."

"I am sorry for your loss. How did you survive?"

"Survive?" Béla considered that question. "How to survive? I go on with life. I have a new wife. A daughter. A business… much to be thankful for."

"So what do you do for a living, Mr. Izsák?"

"I'm a furrier."

"Do you work for yourself?"

"In America, no. But in Israel I have my own shop. It's closed while I spend a year in America."

"You'll never make any money that way."

"So tell me the right way, Professor."

"Sell the business in Israel and invest the money in the stock market."

Béla gave a quizzical look. "And if the market goes poof?"

"The market always comes back. It has to. It's essential to capitalism."

"Maybe you are right," answered Béla. "Maybe America will do business with China now. China is a big country. China can buy televisions and radios from America. I don't know what China can sell to America. They eat rice there. Maybe America can buy rice from China."

The Professor laughed. Just then the train pulled into the Porter Square station. The Professor stood up. "My stop." He held out his hand. "See you around, Mr. Izsák."

"Thank you for the advice about money," Béla called after him.

They did continue to see each other. First on the train, usually in the morning, sometimes in the afternoon, then they eventually had dinner together with Fanny who was always asking questions about investing since she was the one who actually took care of what money the Izsáks did have; just as she had in Bucharest; just as she had when they started out in Israel; just as she did in Rehovot, in Philadelphia and now in Waltham. Because she was smart and listened to the professor's answers, she became a very canny investor and cleverly developed skills that eventually created an even more comfortable life for herself and her family. For his part, the professor was compensated for his advice because he enjoyed listening to Béla's adventures, opinions and philosophy on life.

Meanwhile, Fanny and Béla spent as much time with Rita and her husband as each of their busy schedules would allow. During one weekend visit when Rita and Arie drove from Buffalo to Waltham to pick up Béla and Fanny to vacation together in Cape Cod, they were all gathered in a cozy pub for dinner and drinks. It was cold outside, but inside there was a crackling fire, roasted chestnuts and hot cider. Rita looked relaxed, with a blush of red on her warm round cheeks, and Arie was in an expansive mood talking about his plans for the future when he would finally finish his education and develop a successful career as an architect.

At some point in the conversation, Béla turned to Rita and said, "And you, my big brain daughter. What will you do?"

His question was met with a long silence. All three turned toward Rita, who sat with her mouth open ready to answer but no words came out. Finally she said, "I…I…" A longer pause. Her lower lip trembled. "I still want to have children." And then tears came rolling down her apple cheeks. She stood abruptly and left the fireside table. As Béla watched her, she ran to the front door and fled outside without a coat, hat or scarf. Arie pulled back his chair, but Béla stopped him. "I will go to her," he said. "My words hurt her."

When he caught up with Rita in the parking lot, she was shivering, her lips quivering uncontrollably from the cold and her intense emotions. Béla wrapped his arms around her and whispered, "I am sorry, Rita." But his words only seemed to draw out more tears as she shook in his arms. "Come inside, Rita. Out here, you will freeze."

"I don't care," she sniffled,

"You will be sick."

"Good, then maybe I'll die," she blurted out as she tried to catch her breath in the cold.

Béla was shocked. He had never heard her say anything remotely like that.

Rita turned toward Béla. When she saw the look on his startled face, she shook her head, forced herself to stop crying and calmed down. "I didn't mean that, *Tata*," she said to him in Romanian. Then in English, "I'm just tired."

In the summer, Fanny and Béla returned to Israel, but both of them left with even greater concerns about Rita. Meanwhile, during the following years, instead of starting a career in architecture, Arie added a doctoral degree from Carnegie-Mellon University in Pittsburgh, and later accepted a faculty appointment at the University of Pennsylvania in Philadelphia. As she dutifully followed Arie from College Station to Buffalo to Pittsburg to Philadelphia, Rita continued her own studies, the coursework and exams toward a doctoral degree, but did not finish her dissertation. Compared to Arie who advanced through these career-building phases in a sustained, fast-pace, Rita's progress was slowed by the distress following each miscarriage.

In 1977, Fanny was able to return to the University of Pennsylvania a second time. Béla again closed Béla Furs to travel with Fanny for her year in

Philadelphia. With Arie and Rita both working at the University of Pennsylvania, the families were actually neighbors in the City of Brotherly Love for the next year.

By this point, Rita and Arie had given up on Rita's ability, for whatever reason, to carry a child to term, so they began the long and arduous process of adopting a child. Fanny and Béla were delighted with Rita's decision. They believed that not only would Rita finally have the child she desperately wanted, but that adoption would mean no more difficult pregnancies that were seriously endangering her health.

Because neither Rita nor Arie were US citizens at that time, it was impossible for them to adopt within the United States. Instead, they pursued different possibilities for adoption from foreign countries, but even that process was fraught with frustration and complications. By the time Fanny's third sabbatical year in the US was coming to a close, Rita had still not received any positive news about a baby available for adoption. Unlike the previous times, when Béla would express his strong desire to remain in the US and Fanny would insist that they return to Israel on account of various advantages and assets that they had there, this time Fanny was also not eager to return to Rehovot. This time, it was becoming clear that Rita was committed to making a life in the United States and would not return to Israel. However, as events unfolded, it was fortunate that they had returned to Israel by the time Rita received the news that a set of Columbian twins, a boy and a girl, had been born to a teenaged mother who could not care for them, and that they were therefore available for Rita and Arie to adopt.

Rita immediately responded that they wanted both babies, but taking custody of the babies was not simply a matter of going to Columbia and picking them up. Necessary paperwork had to be provided, which in the case of Rita and Arie was complicated to obtain because of their unconventional backgrounds. Since Arie was born in a Displaced Persons camp in Germany after his parents were liberated from Bergen-Belsen, and Rita was born in Communist Romania, it required numerous trips to consulates in Washington D.C., to request and to track down and obtain their birth certificates, then have these translated from German and Romanian, first into English and then into Spanish, along with notary stamps and Apostille red ribbons. A copy of their Israeli marriage license also had to be translated from Hebrew to English to Spanish. Then, there were home inspections from social workers, and affidavits from their jobs and their physicians, as well as recommendations from their employers and friends. Only then, after four months had passed, Rita and Arie were able to make the trip to Columbia to pick up the infants.

The babies were beautiful. Both Rita and Arie fell immediately in love with them, but they were still required to spend one month in Colombia and submit to interviews by judges, city officials and the Mother Superior of the orphanage.

Things were advancing smoothly until, in one interview with the Mother Superior, after responding to many questions—about their backgrounds and financial situation and plans for caring for the children—the same questions they were asked by many other officials, she asked an unexpected question: "What is your religion?"

Dreading the implications of this question, Rita replied in almost-inaudible whisper, "We are Jewish." After all that they went through to get there, after all the money that they had spent, after growing attached to these babies, to lose everything only because they were Jewish?

"Wonderful," exclaimed the Mother Superior.

Incredulous, confused, Rita asked, "Wonderful?"

"It is wonderful if you will raise the children to believe and to respect God. It doesn't matter what religion. It matters that the children will have a religion."

Allowed, finally, to leave with the little boy and the little girl, Rita and Arie assumed their ordeal was over when they landed in Miami, Florida, on route to their home in Philadelphia.

Instead, when they passed through US immigration they were sent to wait in the area reserved for non-US citizens. This procedure occurred whenever they returned from overseas travel back to the US and was, at first, no cause for concern. Then, as the wait grew longer, Arie approached an official to ask how long they would have to wait since they had two infants with them who needed to be fed and cared for. The official curtly ordered Arie to return to his seat. When Arie began to protest this treatment, the official barked that, "If he didn't return to his seat, he might just end up in the waiting room until hell freezes over." Arie erupted into an angry tirade, but Rita begged him to just sit down and help her with the babies, which he did, although he was still fuming.

After another hour, they were ushered into a sparse office and told by a very stern, middle-aged woman in uniform that since they were not US citizens, they were, "not allowed to bring aliens [the twins] into the country and they must leave immediately!" No appeals, arguments, or presentation of official adoption papers could persuade the immigration official to relent. Eventually she grew tired of talking, and simply said, "You have one hour to arrange a flight out of the country or you will be involuntarily placed on a flight back to Columbia." Then she told them to leave her office and return to the waiting room.

Meanwhile the babies were getting hungry and cranky, and the only thing

Arie and Rita could think to do, was to have Rita and the twins board a flight to Israel, while Arie remained in the US where he would telephone Béla and Fanny that Rita and the babies were coming to Israel. Then, he would try and break through the bureaucratic nightmare when he arrived in Philadelphia, so that Rita could return to the US with the children.

Poor babies and poor Rita. The 17-hour flight to Israel, that also included a stopover in Brussels, came on the heels of the earlier 5-hour flight from Columbia and the wait at the Miami airport, and Rita, who grew up without siblings and had never done any babysitting, had to tend on her own to two tired and irritable babies. Somehow, she and her twins survived the nightmare, but when they landed in Israel, Rita had to brace herself to deal with the Israeli authorities.

Rita, as an Israeli citizen was allowed to stay in Israel, but what of her children? What visa should they be given? They were not, technically, fully legally adopted since there was a one-year period before the adoption became official. So they couldn't be given a family visa. They couldn't be given student visas since they were not students. As the Israeli immigration officials debated this problem in their typical protracted manner, the babies were exhausted and getting colds from the long journey, and Rita was exasperated, screaming at the blasé officials. Finally, it was decided that the children could be granted 3-month tourist visas. Soon after, Fanny and Béla were given custody of their grandchildren and Rita could start being a mother, but it would require several more tourist visa extensions before Rita and her children would be allowed to return to the United States.

Truth be told, Béla and Fanny were not altogether unhappy about having Rita and their grandchildren live with them in Rehovot. They loved the babies, helped care for them, and smothered them with hugs and kisses. It was apparent to Rita that Béla was showering these grandchildren with patient attention and the intense tenderness that he seemed incapable of showing to Rita when she was a young child or even a young adult. Understandably, he was busier in the earlier years and he was coping with many hardships, but it was evident that over the years he had mellowed, was becoming less awkward and less rigid.

When the time came for Rita and the children to return to the United States, Béla and Fanny made the decision that they would follow soon after.

(above left) Béla with grandchildren, Amir and Tali Schinnar, in 1982, at home in Philadelphia.

(above right) Béla getting help from grandson Amir to blow out the birthday candles, in 1983.

(below) Béla with grandson Amir, in 2001.

(above) Béla with Rita and granddaughter Tali at home in Philadelphia, in 1984.

(right) Amir and Tali Schinnar, going off to college in 1995, leaving their whippet puppy at home.

Chapter Nineteen: Retirement

Di tsayt iz tayerer fun gelt.
Time is more precious than money.
— Bernstein, Jüdische Sprichwörter und Redensarten.

After Béla and Fanny moved to the US permanently, Fanny returned again to the University of Pennsylvania's Department of Biochemistry and Biophysics. By this time, the focus of her work changed from research on photosynthesis to research on mitochondria and later research on muscle contraction. Photosynthesis involves the process by which plant cells convert sunlight into energy to support plant life. Mitochondria are the structures in animal cells that break down organic foods to release energy to support the functions of respiration and muscle contraction. In both photosynthesis and cell mitochondria, ATP (adenosine triphosphate) is the molecule that stores energy and releases energy needed for the functions of life. Studies of these processes continue to be intense subjects for scientific research.

Béla immediately found work at an upscale establishment, B&B Furs, in Cherry Hill, New Jersey. The owners were delighted to have such a charming, hard-working employee. His energy level had not diminished and neither had his level of enthusiasm, notwithstanding his age. Others at age 67 might be looking to retire, but Béla was looking forward to continuing to work and even looking forward to having to prove himself, once again, to a new employer. The owners often rewarded Béla with a bottle of Moët & Chandon or Veuve Clicquot upon completion of challenging job orders, along with compliments that "Béla is a good man." The initial remorse Béla experienced because he was no longer his own boss of his own shop, evaporated in the air of hard work, expanded family and the new friends he somehow managed to introduce into his life.

Béla had always been a collector of surprising and unexpected friends. Years earlier, in Israel, when the family was still living in the exceedingly modest stables apartment, Béla once somehow coaxed an opera singer from Tel Aviv to come home with him for dinner.

Fanny and Rita were just getting ready to eat a light meal, when suddenly they heard Béla at the front door conversing in a loud voice with another person. Before they could figure out what was happening, the door flew open and Béla dramatically entered the apartment as he flourished an arm through the air and announced, "Presenting Maestro Boris Hersh, straight from the Tel Aviv Opera to sing for Madam Fanny and her lovely daughter Rita!"

At that moment, a rather heavy-set man wearing a black cloak and sparkling white tuxedo shirt burst into the room and began singing a magnificent, full-throated rendition of *Rio Rita* from the 1927 American musical of the same name.

> *Rio Rita, life is sweeter, Rita, when you are near!*
> *Rio Rita, life's completer, Rita, to have you here…*

Rita dropped a wooden bowl on the floor. Tomatoes and oranges and grapes rolled across the floor while Fanny simply stood in wide-eyed, jaw-dropping amazement, unable to move or say anything at all.

No one ever figured out how Béla convinced a stranger to sing for them in their Rehovot stable apartment located at the edge of town rather than entertaining a sophisticated crowd at a Tel Aviv dinner party. Béla somehow managed to charm people in unexpected ways.

As Béla settled into his later years, an older man with a young heart, he continued to engage with all sorts of people. One evening the doorbell rang, and when Fanny went to answer it, she was introduced to two elderly, impeccably dressed Philadelphia Main Line gentlemen whom Béla had invited to have dinner with them.

When Fanny was able to lure Béla into the kitchen on the pretext that she needed his help to serve the appetizers, she frowned and said, "You told me you were inviting a couple."

"They are a couple," said Béla.

"Oh," said Fanny. She thought for a moment. "Oh…Ooooh."

"They've been together 40 years."

"Oh."

"I met Joel at the newsstand where I buy my Romanian and Israeli newspapers."

"Okay."

"You remember, Fanny. The newsstand in mid-town. The one owned by

Massri."

"Who is Massri?"

"That Arab guy, from Lebanon."

"You're friends with an Arab?"

"He's a good guy. He's just like me."

"An Arab just like you?"

"Just like. Could be my brother."

Dinner with Joel and his partner Mark was a great success, and Fanny had a good time. The Gay Gentlemen from Gladwyne, as Fanny often referred to Mark and Joel, reciprocated by inviting Béla and Fanny to their home.

The walls were covered with art. Béla particularly liked a very colorful village scene that reminded him of Romania. When he told Mark how much he liked the painting, Mark said, "A Chagall. He's not Romanian, though."

"He paints dreams," observed Béla.

"He's a Jew from Lithuania," said Mark.

"Beautiful," said Béla.

Béla, who used to bring home paintings he bought in the Tel Aviv flea market, thought he might buy one as a present for Fanny. He asked, "How much for one of those?"

Mark smiled. "We bought this one a long time ago. I think we picked it up for…" He turned to Joel. "…wasn't it twenty-five?"

Béla was delighted.

"I think it was less than twenty-five thousand," said Joel, "but it must be worth over $100,000 today."

Béla gasped in spite of himself. Fanny poked him in the ribs, hoping he wouldn't say more.

"Well, however much we paid, I think it looks gorgeous hanging over the Bauhaus cabinet, don't you, Fanny?"

Fanny nodded. The painting was beautiful. The cabinet, as well. The entire house was the most beautiful Fanny had ever seen outside a magazine.

During dinner, Fanny remembered an evening back in Israel, a long time ago, when the family went to the movie theater on a Saturday night after a day at the beach. Before the movie began, a man entered the theater and was looking for an empty seat, when some young men in the audience began to call him names, shout and embarrass the man with whistles and catcalls. Béla suddenly stood and angrily yelled at the audience to be quiet and leave the man alone. At the time, Fanny and Rita were embarrassed by Béla's outburst in defense of the man being harassed, a man well known to like other men. Now, looking back, she was proud of what Béla had done, and she smiled at him across the table, although Béla had no idea why she was smiling.

Yet, for all of the good times Béla was having with his life in America, there were also difficult times, mostly centered on the increasing tension between Arie and Rita.

Béla had been convinced that once Rita had children to care for and Arie embraced the joy and pride of fatherhood, they would "grow closer," as relatives had predicted would happen with Béla and Fanny. But Arie, a charming, intelligent, free-spirited man found it difficult to settle into a traditional life.

And raising twins was not easy, even if they were cute and bright and loving. Rita found herself exhausted and edgy at the end of the day even though she had help from Fanny and Béla. By the time that Rita realized that she was not sufficiently attentive to Arie, Arie had already realized that he could get the attention that he craved from someone else.

During a weekend visit to the Philadelphia Zoo, located in a beautiful spot on the west bank of the Schuylkill River, Béla's small grandchildren were watching the baboons cavort around their enclosure built to resemble the African savannah, when Rita suddenly turned to Béla and blurted out that she "just couldn't take it anymore."

Béla, who liked Arie and also was close friends with Arie's parents, was torn between urging Rita to work things through with Arie, and protecting his daughter who was clearly distraught.

"With your big brain and his big brain, you can't make things better?"

"It's not about our brains, *Tăticule* (concatenating Romanian and Yiddish for the endearment term, Daddy). He wants a divorce," she said. Then more softly, "I think I do too."

At that moment, the children grew tired of the baboons, and they ran over to Rita and Béla. The little boy held out his arms to Rita and she lifted him up and gave him a tight hug while the little girl wrapped herself around her grandfather's neck and planted a big kiss on Béla's cheek.

Rita and Arie did get a divorce. Almost concurrently with the divorce, they and their twins appeared together in the Philadelphia Immigration Court, to be sworn in as American citizens. They celebrated the joyful event together, and then turned away from each other to rebuilt separate lives for themselves. Arie resigned from his tenured position at Wharton and moved to California.

Rita eventually started dating again, and both Béla and Fanny acted like they were the parents of a teenager. When they met any of Rita's dates, they were quick to pass judgment as they reviewed each man's qualities and the prospects they offered to give Rita a good life.

A geologist from Europe who was a visiting professor at the University of

California at Berkeley, with whom Rita corresponded and met once, was very congenial, until he made clear that he wished for Rita and her children to return to Europe with him. Another interesting academic, a historian from Cornell University, was agreeable, until outbursts that got ugly. A lawyer from Florida was acceptable, until Rita discovered his preference for quirky sex. A nice Jewish man, a pharmacologist working for Wyeth Pharmaceuticals, a sharp-minded, sharp-tongued Mensa man with a distinguished military career in the Special Forces, was very desirable, until Rita saw hanging above his huge water bed the large black flag with white skeleton and the menacing words, *"If you mess with the best, You die like the rest."* A hippy poet from Chicago was scary, although his poetry captivated Rita's fancy for some time. An environmental engineer with a lucrative private consulting firm looked promising, but he so dominated the conversations that Rita felt suffocated. A very likeable pulmonary physician, with a front-row subscription to the Philadelphia Academy of Music, fell from favor because he would often respond to emergency calls from hospitals and nursing homes, leaving Rita alone at the concerts. And an Israeli physicist and engineer who was the most favored and most fun, lost favor when one day out of the blue, his wife called and accused Rita of stealing her husband, after he had given Rita the impression that he was divorced.

Ultimately, Rita started seeing only one man, Erling Boe, a tall, dignified, Norwegian-American who was also smart and stable, and a tenured professor at the University of Pennsylvania. He was kind and loving to Rita, and the only fault that Fanny and Béla could find in him was that he wasn't Jewish. But Rita married him anyway.

Erling Boe did not convert to Judaism. But after a long courtship, when Erling agreed to change his middle name, Edward, to the more appealing name, Mr. Flexibility, he transformed himself from the somewhat remote and rigid person that he once was (common traits for Norwegians), into a relaxed and emotionally accessible new person, and this change helped this marriage (Erling's third and Rita's second) to work out well.

Béla's next challenge came when the owners of B&B Furs reasoned that they had worked long enough and decided to sell their business and move to Florida where they could lounge in the sun year-round and enjoy their retirement. For a few days, Béla considered buying the business, but on the morning when he planned to make an offer, he looked in the bathroom mirror while he was shaving and saw the usual happy face looking back at him, but the face had white hair and tired eyes. "The apple looks nice on the outside, but is decayed inside," he mumbled to himself. He accepted the fact that he was too old to be running a business, so he abandoned his plan to buy B&B Furs and decided to go into retirement himself. He was 84 years old.

Béla was surprised to discover that retirement actually agreed with him. He spent even more time reading and keeping up with what was happening in the world. He read the Hebrew newspapers for updates on the wars in Lebanon and the First Intifada, mumbling to himself in Yiddish, "*Es iz shver tsu zayn a id!* (It is hard to be a Jew!)" He read the Hungarian papers about the collapse of the Communist regime in Budapest, and the Romanian papers about the dictator Ceaușescu's downfall. And he read in the New York Times and Newsweek about President Reagan and President Clinton and the First War in Iraq.

On the television he watched programs from the History channel and the National Geographic channel, and when Erling came home from work in the evenings, Béla would ask him questions about the origin of the Earth ("I don't believe that all these amazing things were created by God in just six days"); about the technology that makes it possible for airplanes to fly and for ships not to sink ("Tell me, my son-in-law, how is it possible?"); about the original European settlements in America ("Unbelievable! I never heard that the Vikings discovered America before Christopher Columbus. But I know that the Indians were here before Columbus and I know that they died from the new diseases that the Europeans brought to America"); about UFOs ("Tell me, my son-in-law, do YOU believe this?"); and about many more subjects that he never had a chance to learn in school, because his mother had to send him to learn a trade when he was young so that he would be able to support himself when he was older.

Some of the complicated stuff about scientific and medical advances that Béla learned on television and was very impressed by, did not translate into practical understanding. When Béla was 92 years old and was scheduled for a cataract operation on one eye, he called Israel to chat with his 90 years old brother, Sanyi, about this surgery. After this conversation, Béla was relieved, because his brother explained to him that a cataract operation was not really surgery. "They wash the eye. They wash it and clean it really well. It is just a very special eye wash." Neither the ophthalmologist who had talked with Béla, nor the television program that Béla saw, provided such a simple, straightforward explanation that Béla could easily understand and believe was credible.

Béla actually paid attention to television ads. He thought he could benefit from losing some weight.

"I should get this surgery that they advertise on television which cuts part of the stomach," he told Rita.

"It would be easier if you just stopped eating so many cookies," Rita answered.

"No. The surgery will be easier…," Béla insisted.

Béla, in retirement, also joined Fanny and Rita on visits to the Philadelphia Museum of Art, where Sylvester Stallone ran up and down the steps in the iconic film, *Rocky*, and to the Pennsylvania Academy of Fine Arts, where Béla stood for a long time to admire *The Cello Player*, an oil painting by Thomas Eakins. At the Brandywine Museum in Chadds Ford, Pennsylvania, Béla admired the paintings of three generations of the Wyeth family (N.C. Wyeth, Andrew Wyeth, and James Wyeth), and he bought many postcards to be reminded of his visit there.

He listened to music, even to classical music concerts, and he watched ballet performances and opera performances on television. He admired talent. "Brain is brain!" he would remark with appreciation, using a simple expression to communicate the essence of his observation that when someone has a gifted and capable brain, this shows. "It's not a simple thing," he would declare, respecting and admiring a creative work by an artist, or an architect, or some feat of engineering, as well as an outstanding performance by a dancer, opera singer, or music conductor. "Man is God!" he decreed.

He played in the park with his grandchildren when they were little and he enjoyed their company. After they left home to go away to college, he was proud of them and trusted that they were on their best behavior there too. To anyone who would listen, Béla would brag that, "My grandchildren don't take drugs, don't drink alcohol, don't do sex." If the kids were around to hear this, they would nod in mock agreement and would chuckle. But Béla believed this. He would also add, "May God preserve their good habits."

And Béla continued to collect more friends.

One afternoon while he was buying his Hungarian newspaper from Massri, a young man named Matt introduced himself and asked Béla if he was Hungarian. When Béla said that he was, the young man asked Béla if they could meet from time to time and speak Hungarian.

"But Matt, why would a guy like you want to speak this crazy language?" asked Béla.

"Because I'm going to attend medical school there," replied the young man.

"Why do you have to go so far when you have good schools in Philadelphia?"

"Because I wasn't accepted to any American medical colleges. Many international students go to Hungary. I am going to the University of Debrecen."

"I heard of Debrecen. It is near Transylvania where I was born," said Béla. "When you finish school there, can you work in America?"

"Yes, but only after I pass some exams here."

"Well, *Akkor kezdjük* (let us begin)…," Béla said to Matt. And Matt, not only finished medical school in Hungary, he also married a young Hungarian woman studying psychiatry and, later, they had a little girl. They would arrange to meet Béla whenever they returned to Philadelphia for a visit.

Then, on one brisk but beautiful autumn morning, not long after he celebrated his 86th birthday, Béla woke up feeling like he did when he banged his head on the iron sink back in Israel. When he tried to get out of bed, he found he could barely move. Béla, who never showed fear, was afraid. He tried to call out to Fanny and tell her how he was feeling, but he couldn't form the words properly. When Fanny heard his incoherent mumbling, she immediately realized Béla was in serious distress. She called an ambulance and they rushed Béla to the hospital.

Hours passed. Rita joined Fanny in the emergency waiting room. Finally, a young doctor approached them. "Are you here for Adalbert Izsák?"

When they both nodded, the doctor tried to put on a cheerful expression, but he couldn't manage to look sincere in his attempt. "Mr. Izsák has had a serious stroke," the doctor told them. Fanny became very upset. Rita was in shock. "But he was…"

Fanny interrupted her. "Will he talk? Will he walk? Will he know…?" She couldn't continue.

The doctor shrugged. "The next few days will tell us what the effects of his stroke will bring, but…"

"But what?" asked Rita.

"He's an old man," said the doctor. "We will hope for the best, of course, but we should anticipate…uh…problems."

But what the doctors didn't anticipate was the courage and determination of Béla's spirit. Within weeks he had pushed himself to get out of bed on his own. He began to speak coherently. Not long after, he was walking again albeit with a cane. Fortunately for him, he experienced no slack facial expressions, no drooping mouth, no dimming of his eyes, no permanent speech impairment, no memory loss, no lethargy of the soul. It was another amazing Béla performance.

And yet, he would lament that "Age is unforgiving," and he would be melodramatic and funny about this. "*Greu la deal* (It's difficult climbing uphill)," he would complain in Romanian.

"What hurts you?" Fanny asked him.

"You ask what hurts me? You should ask what doesn't hurt me? I am a sick man!"

"You are not a sick man. You are just old," Fanny answered in jest.

"You are right. Nothing really hurts me. I just feel the weakness of old age."

He invented a rhyme in Romanian, *"Haine grele, ce să fac cu ele?* (Heavy old clothes, what am I to do with those?)", and later added a second rhyme, *"Haine grele, cum să scap de ele?* (Heavy old clothes, how am I to get rid of those?)."

Each day, at home, he would climb the three flights leading from the first floor to the second floor, and as he reached the landing, he would exclaim: "This is Mount Everest. If I can climb this, then I'm Tarzan, for sure." He would complain about the effort, and yet he was proud of himself for being able to do it. It was a strain, not a struggle. Fanny and Rita knew this because Béla, invariably, laughed when he made those declarations. He was in a good mood and he made Fanny and Rita laugh. In fact, the humor that would turn up unexpectedly and his unique expressions, some borrowed and some that he made up himself on the spur of the moment, were more visible in his old age.

When Fanny once caught Béla in the act of dipping into her jar of expensive face cream, he explained that, "I was thinking to myself that if this cream works so well for you and Rita, it can't hurt me."

"So you've been doing this for a while?" asked Fanny. "I wondered why my face cream seemed to go so quickly."

"Yes. For some time. It is really good cream," Béla offered.

"Well, in truth, it seems to be working better on you than on either Rita or me," Fanny remarked but then added, "I'll get you a cheaper face cream. This one is too expensive."

"I am such a bad thief. I always get caught," Béla concluded with resignation.

After his rehabilitation, Béla was conflicted between his intense desire to socialize and his embarrassment that people would see him walk slowly with a cane. He solved his dilemma by taking early morning walks to a bench in the Penn's Landing waterfront park overlooking the Delaware River, an area that he declared to be, "My Hawaii." There he sat each day enjoying years of providing unsolicited but appreciated advice, ridiculous interventions into other people's lives that mostly worked out for the best, and unlikely match-making that resulted in one lasting and happy marriage.

One summer morning, while he was sitting with his eyes apparently closed as he basked in the warm sunlight, his face lathered with rich emollient to protect his skin, a woman passed by whom he recognized from his neighborhood. Béla had long admired this woman with the slim, physically-fit figure and short, curly silver hair that framed an attractive face with sparkling eyes. Béla's eyes snapped open and he engaged her in a conversation about nothing in particular. When he found out her name was Barbara, he said, "Barbara, look how I keep my arms strong!" as he demonstrated his famous 'Béla shoulder presses' with his cane. He was delighted when she laughed, and he giggled along with her.

That initial conversation evolved into a long-standing friendship. She would always stop if she saw him sitting on his bench and give him an enthusiastic greeting, including a kiss on his cheek that usually resulted in Sáring his skin cream on her own face. He told her stories about his long life, his tragic memories from World War II, his amazing adventures and his career as a furrier, always adding that what he loved most about his profession was making beautiful garments for beautiful women, said in such a frank, unabashed way that his admissions only increased his charm.

In return, Barbara showered Béla with small gifts—CDs with Yiddish songs, Hungarian songs, and Romanian and Russian folk ballads. She even hired a talented young harpist to play at Béla's 94th birthday party, that turned out to be his last party before he went into the hospital again, although at the time, he was full of excitement and fully engaged with his guests.

Béla also became close friends with Robert, a middle-aged man who looked much younger, a former model who kept in shape by working out at the gym. Robert was one of those unique characters who was clearly smart and articulate, although mostly self-educated, and who seemed to possess various unexpected talents, including a hilarious capacity to mimic accents and ethnic stereotypes that he used to entertain Béla, who would laugh appreciatively each time Robert unravelled another tall tale.

Robert treated Béla as if he were the father Robert no longer had and, in return, Béla saw Robert as the son he wished that he had sired. They were demonstratively affectionate with each other. Robert would regularly pick up the local Metro newspaper from a corner street box and, on his way to the office each morning, would deliver the paper to Béla who was always looking forward to this encounter. Béla would beam with pleasure when he saw Robert approach, and Robert would plant a kiss on Béla's shiny forehead.

One day, Robert told Béla an especially funny story, mimicking a Jewish accent, although Robert was not Jewish:

> An old Jewish man was finally allowed to leave the Soviet Union, to emigrate to Israel. When he was searched at the Moscow airport, the customs official found a bust of Lenin.
>
> Customs official: What is that?
>
> Old man: What is that? What is that?! Don't say "What is that?" Say "Who is that?" That is Lenin! The genius who thought up this workers' paradise!
>
> The official laughed and let the old man through.

> The old man arrived at Tel Aviv airport, where an Israeli customs official found the bust of Lenin.
>
> Customs official: What is that?
>
> Old man: What is that? What is that?! Don't say "What is that?" Say "Who is that?" That is Lenin! The son of a bitch! I will put him on display in my toilet for all the years he prevented an old man from coming home.
>
> The official laughed and let him through.
>
> When he arrived at his family's house in Jerusalem, his grandson saw him unpack the bust.
>
> Grandson: Who is that?
>
> Old man: Who is that? Who is that?! Don't say "Who is that?" Say "What is that?" That, my child, is eight pounds of gold.

Béla laughed and giggled for a long time because he could appreciate the political nuance as well as the sarcasm involving Jewish cunning. Although he appreciated all of Robert's stories and his daily visits, on that day he spontaneously took his watch off his wrist and gave it to Robert. Robert accepted Béla's gift and wore Béla's watch as if it were an inheritance from his father.

Another friend, Steve, a professional man in his mid-forties, a married man with a warm and lively personality, was also very attentive to Béla. Béla so liked the attention that he received from Steve, that he would often confide to him about vague aches in his shoulder or his knee, confident that Steve would be responsive and surprise him, as indeed he always had, with some soothing cream to try to alleviate these "pains of old age," as Béla referred to them.

Steve once described to Rita the nature of their friendship. "Béla would grab your arm and say, 'Now, Steve, let me tell you…,' and it could be about anything. Of course, Béla was Old World, eastern European, where it was a sign of friendship and affection for two males to kiss, and we did, in affection and deference to old customs."

Then there was a beautiful, blond, young woman named Eleanor. She rented a small apartment near Penn's Landing, and each morning she would walk her beloved fluffy white Bichon Frise, Blanche DuBois, past Béla who was sitting on his 'Hawaiian' bench. After a time, she and Béla began to talk and Béla told her his stories and she talked to Béla about her life.

On one occasion, Béla asked Eleanor if she had a boyfriend, and Eleanor told him she did not. Her answer seemed to excite Béla who laughed and slapped his hands together declaring, "I know a man! Scott. You must meet him!"

"Why?" asked Eleanor.

"He has a dog!" Béla pointed to Blanche. "He works on the computer." Béla demonstrated, typing on an imaginary keyboard as he nodded in agreement with himself. "He is a good man."

Eleanor was reluctant to agree to a meeting, but Béla was so delighted with the prospect, that she couldn't help but giggle along with him and so she agreed to meet this man with a dog, thinking to herself that if the guy had the love and respect that she did for Béla, then what could be so horrible about meeting him and making Béla happy.

The next morning, Eleanor took Blanche out to the park for her daily walk and as she headed toward Béla's bench, she saw a pair of broad shoulders sitting on the bench facing away from her and toward Béla.

Béla's eyes lit up and he began to chuckle when he saw Eleanor. The shoulders stood up to face her, all 6 foot 4 inches of him, and he smiled at her. "I'm Scott, but I guess you already knew that," he said.

"Hi, I'm Eleanor," she said somewhat shyly although she was not normally a shy person.

They shook hands. Scott made room for her on the bench and Béla moved to the opposite bench, where he swung his feet in youthful delight.

Scott and Eleanor talked for almost two hours, and after a while, they didn't even notice Béla anymore. A few months later, Scott proposed to Eleanor. A year after their meeting was arranged by Béla, they were married. As Béla would remark to Rita, "I am not telling people what to do. I am just saying maybe they should. Saying is different from telling…" Béla lived on to see two of the three children that Scott and Eleanor eventually had together.

Seeing the success that he had with Scott and Eleanor, Béla got it into his head that he should try to arrange another successful merger between another young man and another young woman that he had befriended in his 'Hawaii.' He went through the same motions to get David, a lawyer in the entertainment business, and Jennifer, a nurse in a local hospital, to agree to show up at the same time at his 'Hawaii,' and they did. Only this time, Béla failed. David pulled Béla aside and whispered in his ear, "If you had only brought me a man…"

When Béla told Rita this story, she advised him that he was not suited for this business because his interviews with people were not sufficiently probing.

There was also Brad, a muscular, handsome Black man who was a dog-walker. Inescapably this meant that Brad would often pass by the bench where Béla was sitting, waiting to "trap" people into conversation and light banter. There was also Sue, a perky young woman who was also a dog-walker who became a cheerful friend of Béla's. Then there was Mauro, a middle-aged, married man from Italy who worked as an airline steward. When he returned from his travels overseas and he would meet Béla, he would stop to give him a kiss on both cheeks and, on special occasions, a holiday or a birthday, he would bring to Béla boxes of chocolate, from *Maxim's De Paris*.

There was also another friend that Béla had met when he'd stop at the Chef's Market Café, not far from his house, to drink a cup of coffee and eat a piece of cake and observe the passers-by on South Street. The young waitress, with long, black hair and delicate porcelain face, was Chinese. Béla learned that her given name was Jia, but in America she preferred to be called Isabella. Jia learned that his given name was Adalbert but everyone called him Béla, and so they developed an easy rapport. Jia was also among the guests to show up for Béla's 94th birthday party, and brought him a beautiful, tall, burgundy-colored orchid. The orchid lasted much longer than the chocolates and longer than Béla.

Age, gender, ethnicity, skin color, professional status, marital status-- none of these made a difference to Béla. He would declare to Rita, "I love people," and people loved him. He was embarrassed to be seen using a cane but couldn't resist socializing.

To understand, perhaps, the effect that Béla had on people, a retired administrative-law judge, Ralph Romano, who also befriended Béla, tried to explain it in these words:

> I'd pass by Béla many times—him sitting in the sun. He looked like my dad and my grandfathers, and I grew up with Italian 'mobsters', totally male and strong.
>
> No matter what my mood at the various times of day, I knew that I must greet Béla, or, better, receive his greeting, which always demanded my attention to be joyful. Béla challenged one to be joyful.
>
> Béla would rise up, and let you know that you were special and recognized as an important person in his life at this moment. Formal, humble, and totally attentive. I'd leave him always feeling that I was a better person.

A painter who liked to wander the waterfront at Penn's Landing, painting pictures of the landscape and the tourists and the boats on the Delaware River, noticed Béla and insisted on painting his portrait. He gave Béla the painting and refused to allow Béla to pay him. Béla added the portrait to his collection of not-so-great art that Fanny didn't particularly care for, but that one she hung on the living room wall because it captured Béla in a reflective mood that he did not often show to the world.

The varied friendships that Béla made so effortlessly, surely, reflected something about him. But these friendships just as surely reflected a special quality in the persons who reciprocated Béla's attentions. These individuals made space in their rushed, busy lives to show kindness to an old man with a cane, with an accent, with a background so different from theirs. Why? Because they shared a capacity for warmth, love, respect, and the courage to express these emotions to another.

And always with him there were Fanny and Rita. They pampered him. Béla often remarked in appreciation, "Fanny, Rita, what the two of you don't do for me!" In phrasing it that way, with his distinctive Hungarian intonation that he added to it, he was expressing amazement and humbleness at receiving so much tender care and attention that he didn't feel he deserved.

Rita's husband, Erling, also strove to please Béla. On weekends, Erling would drive Béla on day trips through the countryside, stopping for lunch at quaint inns and for dinner at charming restaurants nestled in the hills and valleys of rural Pennsylvania. In the evenings, Erling would occasionally pull a chair to sit by Béla's side when he was watching the news on CNN, and engage him in light conversations that Béla enjoyed immensely.

"Now, that's an interesting proposition!" Béla would exclaim when Erling explained something to him that impressed him. Then he would say, "Thank you."

"For what?" asked Erling.

"Because I had the exquisite pleasure to listen to you."

Béla referred to these chats as, "This is Happy Hour," although Erling was the one who was actually drinking a chilled Martini while Béla was only imbibing the words and ideas that Erling was Sáring with him.

In retirement, Béla, no longer working, regularly admonished Rita and Erling to keep working hard.

In the mornings, he would greet Erling with, "My son-in-law, have a good day! Hard work!" And in the evenings, he would welcome Erling with, "My son-in-law, did you have a good day?"

"Yes. I worked hard."

"Good. I am very happy," Béla replied with a satisfied grin.

When Béla was 90 years old, Rita cut back on her work to have even more time to spend with Béla. She loved him with the fierce love she had developed so late in life when she realized how much he meant to her and how much time was running out.

Then, these daily routines, slow-paced, relaxed and pleasant, were disturbed when he checked into a hospital on August 4, 2006, to correct a problem with his enlarged prostate. The doctors explained that it was a simple procedure that would require an overnight's stay in the hospital. Béla's spirits were good. He summoned all of his strength and optimism. "Here we go again," he whispered to himself as he vowed to fight once more.

But this time the odds were stacked too highly against him. He was 94 years old, after all. It was four months since the big birthday party that Fanny and Rita arranged with so many of his young friends who came to celebrate with him, friends who made him feel so special and honorable. "I did a few things in my life," Béla mused to himself, thinking about the long span and the strange arc of his life as he entered the hospital for the last time.

(top left) Béla at 45 in 1957.
(top right) Béla at 54 in 1966.
(left) Béla at 72 in 1984. Over the years, his hairline receded, his face became fuller, and the girth became wider, very different from the scrawny man who delivered ice blocks when he immigrated to Israel in 1950.
(next page top left) Béla at 83 in 1995, a content grandfather attending the high-school graduation of his grandchildren, Amir and Tali.
(next page top right) Béla at 88 in 2000, somewhat pensive shortly after a stroke.
(next page bottom left) Béla at 93 in 2005, with his signature wide smile, twinkling eyes, and generally good disposition.
(next page bottom right) Béla at 94 in 2006, looking relaxed and content at his home in Philadelphia, just a few months before he passed away.

Chapter Twenty: The Last Fight

Azoy lang der mentsh lebt iz im di gantse velt tsu kleyn; nokhn toyt iz im der keyver genug.
As long as a man lives, the entire world is too small for him; after death, the grave is big enough.
— Bernstein, Jüdische Sprichwörter und Redensarten.

The surgeon who performed the procedure on Béla decided to 'keep an eye on him' one extra night in the hospital, on account of his age. This was an unfortunate decision because Béla contracted pneumonia that compromised his breathing and weakened him, so what was expected to be a short hospital stay became month-long and then the end of Béla's life on earth.

Béla was transferred to a nearby rehab facility to help him get stronger by a regimen of daily exercises. He was not pleased. He saw the patients with various states of disability and he remarked to Rita, "My heart goes out to these poor people." It amused Rita because he clearly did not seem to see himself as being one of these 'poor people.' He was annoyed by his weakened state, and still he was funny.

When he was asked to stand up and try to throw a ball into a basketball hoop that was placed close to him, he succeeded on the first try. Then, when the physical therapist instructed him to repeat this five more times, Béla just stood there, holding the ball in his hands, pretending to ignore the instructions. The therapist called out Béla's name several times but no response. "What's the matter?" Rita asked. Béla motioned with one hand to move the hoop further away. It was too close, too easy, and he wanted to be challenged. The therapist didn't think it was realistic, but Béla proved him wrong. He continued to throw the ball into the hoop, time after time as it was moved further away, at his insistence.

One late afternoon, as Rita was sitting by Béla's bedside and talking on the telephone with Fanny to give her a progress report on Béla's condition, Béla interrupted the conversation. "Tell your mother that my greatest wish and biggest dream is to get home and have sex with her one more time." To which Fanny replied, "Tell your father that his wish shall remain a dream." Béla laughed. At his age, he was still dreaming, or maybe he was just joking.

He was making good progress. Rita was certain that he would be released soon, and Béla was certain as well. "Rita, what are we waiting for?" he asked every day, and Rita answered, "We are waiting for you to get stronger." "Where is your car, Rita?" he asked, "Because I am thinking to myself that maybe we can just get out of here and go home already."

But near the end of the month, Béla landed back in the hospital. He was weaker and much sicker. And yet, when Rita arrived at the hospital the next morning, on the day that was her birthday, Béla surprised her. He pulled himself up into sitting position and sang: "Happy birthday to you, till you are 120!" Rita tried to shush him, not to disturb the other patients, but Béla was determined to repeat the song a second time, and Rita wondered how he had mustered the strength to do this.

He was also, as usual, stubborn. The doctors wanted Béla to sleep with an oxygen mask at night. Béla would not accept being constrained by the oxygen mask. He would pull hard at it, tear it away from his face, and throw it to the floor. No amount of reasoning that it was important to keep the mask on his face was effective. When Rita would ask the nurses how long he had kept the mask on his face during the night, they complained with frustration, "Are you kidding? Not even fifteen minutes pass before we, again and again, find the mask on the floor."

Even on what would turn out to be the last day, Béla was still stubbornly trying to be independent. When Rita arrived at the hospital very early in the morning, as she had done each day during that awful month, she found Béla half-sitting up in bed. He was very thirsty, he said. It was too early for the breakfast to arrive and the cafeteria was still closed, so a nurse heated tea for him and brought it to his room in a Styrofoam cup. Rita held the hot cup in her hands and tried to bring it carefully to Béla's lips, to help him sip slowly from it. He refused. "I want to hold the cup in my hands," he insisted. Rita tried to persuade him that the Styrofoam cup was not sturdy and in his weakened state he might spill hot water on himself, but he said he could handle it. He solved the problem by slowly and carefully pressing both sides of the flexible Styrofoam to create a funnel, and he sipped from it without spilling.

It had been their routine every morning during this month, for Rita to hand over to Béla his electric shaver so he could shave his beard, then hand him the comb so he could comb his hair, then hand him his favorite shaving lotion, Brute, to sprinkle it on his face and forehead. "It revives me," he said. Then she would hand him the jar of face cream to apply to his face and forehead, "to present a glowing face to the world," he said. The hospital staff appreciated how nicely he looked and he enjoyed receiving the compliments. But on this day, Béla rejected the routine. He did not feel like shaving, he said. This was uncharacteristic of him, perhaps a foreshadowing that grooming was irrelevant to where he was going, but Rita couldn't read the tea leaves. She tried to persuade Béla to change his mind, but he insisted, "Not today. I don't feel like doing it today." So Rita let it pass. Béla closed his eyes to get some more rest.

Soon, however, Béla opened his eyes and seemed agitated. He was disturbed by the television that was hanging from the ceiling. The television was not turned on, but something about that black box bothered him, and he asked Rita to arrange to have it removed from the room. Was this too a foreshadowing? Was Béla already looking into some black box that frightened him? When Rita explained that it was an odd request that couldn't be fulfilled, Béla closed his eyes again.

Soon however, Béla reopened his eyes and this time, with urgency, asked for the electric shaver. He wanted to shave his beard after all. Rita was delighted. He sounded more normal. They proceeded in the usual order, although at a much slower pace than usual, following the steps of the familiar routine from the previous days: Rita handed Béla the shaver and, on his own, he was shaving his face. Then Rita handed him the comb and he combed his hair. Then she handed him the shaving lotion and he applied it to his face and forehead and around his neck, but this time without the usual commentary and without the sparkle in his eyes. Then she handed him the face cream, and Béla remarked that this was actually the expensive cream that Fanny was using, and that she brought this to him to lift his morale in the hospital and to let him know that she thought that he was worth it. Then, when he was finished spreading the smooth silky face cream over his face and big forehead, he asked for the mirror, inspected the outcome, smiled with contentment at the image staring back at him, and declared himself to be "A New Man." Was this also a foreshadowing?

Then, immediately after, Béla fell asleep. Rita picked up a newspaper and sat by his bedside to read. The room was quiet, Béla seemed calm. With luck, they might leave this place soon.

Suddenly, a nurse rushed into the room and, without saying a word, proceeded to turn off the monitors and whatever equipment that was buzzing.

It startled Rita. "Why are you doing this?"

"It's over," the nurse answered.

Rita didn't understand. "What do you mean it's over?"

"He is gone."

Rita looked at Béla. His face was relaxed and handsome. "How can it be over?" It was exactly 10:30am.

The nurse encouraged Rita to stay in the room, "because his spirit was still hovering there," she said. Rita accepted that. For the next three hours she just stood by the side of the bed and continually caressed Béla's smooth forehead. He felt warm and looked peaceful.

When Rita walked out from the hospital, her eyes blurred from crying, her heart broken into bits, a part of her mind accepted that old age ends like this. This is the way of the world, all things come to an end. Yet, another part of her was disturbed by the thought that, were it not for the unexpected development of acquiring the pneumonia in the hospital, Béla might have lived a while longer. After all, he used to tell everyone, "I have a contract with Rita to live until 120."

Obviously, God had nullified their contract.

(above) Béla with Harvey, and (below) Béla with Stewart.

(above) Béla with Dan and Dana and little Sam.

(left) Béla with a young lovely new friend.

(below) Béla with Matt and his Hungarian wife.

(above) Béla with Phil.

(right) Béla with Eleanor in 1991.

(below) Béla with Nicole and little Matthew.

(above) Béla with Robert, and (below) Béla with more friends in 2004.

Epilogue

Seventy two years have passed since Béla's mother, Stefánia Izsák, his brother, Yaakov, and his wife, Sári, were rounded up by the Nazis from their village in Gâlgău, along with 1600 additional Jewish men, women and children from the neighboring towns around Gherla, Transylvania, then part of Hungary. They were sent in cattle cars to Auschwitz where virtually all perished. A monument dedicated to the memory of these innocent victims was unveiled in a somber ceremony on May 22, 2016, in Gherla, now part of Romania.

If you go on the internet, you may view the Gherla Holocaust Memorial Monument at: *http://gherla-holocaust-memorial.weebly.com*.

It was by sheer chance that the timing of the completion and dedication of the Gherla Holocaust Memorial Monument coincided with the publication of this book. Through these two events—the Gherla Monument on which Stefánia's and Yaakov's names are now engraved and Béla's Story—we are proud to bear witness to the lives of all those who died and who now rise symbolically from the ashes. Their lives have enormous significance for their children, grandchildren, great-grandchildren and the countless other children unto the last generations in time, even if they were temporarily deemed insignificant by the evil that murdered them.

About The Authors

Rita Schinnar: An epidemiologist is what an epidemiologist does, and a writer is what a writer does. Rita Schinnar was, for 38 years, an epidemiologist at the Center for Clinical Epidemiology and Biostatistics in the Perlman School of Medicine of the University of Pennsylvania in Philadelphia. As part of her work, Ms. Schinnar worked on a large number of epidemiologic studies and co-authored papers that were published in medical journals. She was also the Managing Editor and a contributor to several editions of a renowned book and a textbook in Pharmacoepidemiology, and the Managing Editor for the *Journal of Pharmacoepidemiology and Drug Safety.*

When Ms. Schinnar wrote her first scientific paper, the comments she received from peer reviewers noted that the paper was important and interesting but the writing was more suitable for a literary periodical; for a scientific publication, she was told, the writing should be parsimonious and stripped of florid language. The repressed desire for expansive expression had to wait, finally finding an outlet in her current writings... In retirement for the past two years, Ms. Schinnar is a writer of travelogues, short stories and this first memoir.

Ms. Schinnar completed her undergraduate studies in education (at the Levinsky College of Education in Tel Aviv, Israel) and in psychology and European history (at Texas A&M University, in College Station, Texas, and the State University of New York at Buffalo). She completed graduate studies in public administration and policy analysis at the Graduate School of Public and International Affairs at the University of Pittsburgh, Pennsylvania, where she earned a Master's degree and finished doctoral studies, except for a dissertation.

Ms. Schinnar's hobbies include photography and films.
Contact: BelaStory@gmail.com

William A. Meis. Editor, novelist, poet and publisher, Mr. Meis has written numerous books, collaborated on many more, and publishes the **Fallen Bros Press** catalogue of fiction, essays and memoirs. He was the co-founder of the influential international journal, *New Perspectives Quarterly (NPQ)*, and a long-time Director of Publications for the Writers Guild of America (west). He holds an MFA degree from Goddard College, and lives with his wife and young son in Southern California.

Made in the USA
Columbia, SC
30 April 2018